@Copyright 2020by Ben Tuten- **All rights reserved.**

This document is geared towards providing exact and reliable information in regards to the topic and issue covered. The publication is sold with the idea that the publisher is not required to render accounting, officially permitted, or otherwise, qualified services. If advice is necessary, legal or professional, a practiced individual in the profession should be ordered.

Under no circumstance will any legal responsibility or blame be held against the publisher for any reparation, damages, or monetary loss due to the information herein, either directly or indirectly.

Legal Notice:The book is copyright protected. This is only for personal use. You cannot amend, distribute, sell, use, quote or paraphrase any part or the content within this book without the consent of the author.

Disclaimer Notice:Please note the information contained within this document is for educational and entertainment purposes only. Every attempt has been made to provide accurate, up to date and reliable complete information. No warranties of any kind are expressed or implied. Readers acknowledge that the author is not engaging in the rendering of legal, financial, medical or professional advice. The content of this book has been derived from various sources. Please consult a licensed professional before attempting any techniques outlined in this book.

CONTENTS

Ninja Foodi Indoor Grill 5
- Cyclone Grilling 5
- No Necessary Flipping 5
- Cook Anytime 6
- Compact Design 6
- Safe, Easy to Clean, & Economical 6

BREAKFAST 7
- Grilled Bruschetta 7
- Grilled Chicken Tacos 8
- Grilled French Toast 9
- Sausage with Eggs 10
- Espresso Glazed Bagels 10
- Bruschetta Portobello Mushrooms 11
- Avocado Eggs 12
- Coconut French Toast 13
- Bacon-Herb Grit 14
- Toast Kebabs 15

APPETIZERS & SNACKS 15
- Cob with Pepper Butter 15
- Grilled Eggplant 16
- Tarragon Asparagus 17
- Grilled Butternut Squash 17
- Honey Glazed Bratwurst 18
- Chicken Salad with Blueberry Vinaigrette 19
- Pineapple with Cream Cheese Dip 20
- Ninja Grill Hot Dogs 21

VEGETARIAN 22
- Cheddar, Squash And Zucchini Casserole 22
- Roasted Vegetables Salad 23
- Zucchini Parmesan Chips 24
- Zucchini Antipasto 25
- Jalapeño Cheese Balls 25
- Jicama Fries 26
- Sage And Garlic Grilled Tomatoes 27
- Crispy Roasted Broccoli 28
- Creamy And Cheese Broccoli Bake 29
- Coconut Battered Cauliflower Bites 31
- Grilled Eggplant With Feta And Lemon 32
- Crispy Jalapeno Coins 33
- Grilled Brussels Sprouts with Balsamic Glaze 33
- Spaghetti Squash Tots 34
- Buffalo Cauliflower 34
- Crisped Baked Cheese Stuffed Chile Pepper 35
- Jumbo Stuffed Mushrooms 36
- Crispy And Healthy Avocado Fingers 37
- Cinnamon Butternut Squash Fries 37

FISH AND SEAFOOD 38
- Spanish Shrimp 38
- Healthy Fish and Chips 39
- Moroccan Salmon 40
- Quick Paella 41
- Grilled Teriyaki-Glazed Coho Salmon 42
- Cilantro-Lime Fried Shrimp 43
- Halibut 44
- Lemony Tuna 45

Grilled Soy Salmon Fillets 46
Simple Grilled Swordfish 47
Flying Fish 48
"Barbecued" Salmon 49
Pistachio-Crusted Lemon-Garlic Salmon 50
Louisiana Shrimp Po Boy 51
Seared Sea Scallops With Roasted Garlic And Dill Butter 52
Scallops and Spring Veggies 53
Tuna With Fresh Tomato-Basil Sauce 54
Tuna Stuffed Potatoes 55
Salmon Noodles 56
Fried Calamari 57

POULTRY 58
Grilled Stuffed Pork Tenderloin 58
Grill Pork Quesadilla 59
Roasted Pork Tenderloin 60
Italian Parmesan Breaded Pork Chops 61
Korean Spicy Pork 62
Chinese Salt and Pepper Pork Chop Stir-fry 63
Garlic Putter Pork Chops 64
Fried Pork with Sweet and Sour Glaze 64
Molasses BBQ Pork Chops 65
Pork Cutlet Rolls 66
Sweet And Salty Lemongrass Pork Chops 67
Dijon Garlic Pork Tenderloin 68
Air Fryer Sweet and Sour Pork 69
Fried Pork Scotch Egg 70
Roasted Char Siew (Pork Butt) 71
Wonton Taco Cups 72

BEEF PORK AND LAMB 73
Cold Soba With Beef And Cucumber 73
Beef Ribeye Steak 74
Filets Mignons With Gaucho Seasonings 74
Chili-Espresso Marinated Steak 75
Marinated London Broil 76
Cumin-Paprika Rubbed Beef Brisket 77
Beef Bulgogi 77
Smoked Meat Loaf 78
Beef with Pesto 79
Sweet Chipotle Ribs 80
Steak with Salsa Verde 81
Pork with Salsa 82
Sweet Ham Kabobs 83
Steak & Bread Salad 84
Raspberry Pork Chops 85
Cheese Burgers 85
American Burger 86
Basil Pizzas 87
Skewers with Chimichurri 88
Lamb Skewers 89
Korean Flank Steak 90
Fajita Skewers 91

CHICKEN & TURKEY 92
Chicken Fajitas 92
Balsamic-Rosemary Chicken Breasts 93
Orange Curried Chicken Stir-Fry 93

Chicken Paillards With Fresh Tomato Sauce 94
Grilled Chicken Fajitas 95
Honey-Mustard Chicken Tenders 96
Chicken Roast with Pineapple Salsa 97
Mustard Chicken Tenders 97
Tarragon Chicken Tenders 98
Cheesy Chicken in Leek-Tomato Sauce 99
Honey BBQ-Glazed Chicken Drumsticks 100
Marinated Turkey Breast With Cranberry Compote 101
Grilled Chicken With Salsa Criolla 102
Chicken BBQ with Sweet And Sour Sauce 103
Ricotta and Parsley Stuffed Turkey Breasts 104
Sweet Thai Cilantro Chili Chicken Quarters 105
Cheesy Turkey-Rice with Broccoli 106

DESSERT 107

Blueberry Lemon Muffins 107
Grilled Pound Cake with Berry Compote 107
Sweet Cream Cheese Wontons 108
Air Fryer Cinnamon Rolls 108
Smoked Apple Crumble 109
Bread Pudding with Cranberry 110
Black and White Brownies 110
French Toast Bites 111
Baked Apple 111
Coffee And Blueberry Cake 112
Cinnamon Sugar Roasted Chickpeas 112
Cinnamon Fried Bananas 113
Cherry-Choco Bars 113

Ninja Foodi Indoor Grill

Ninja® Foodi™ Grill is nothing but convenience for those who love to enjoy nicely grilled food but too busy to set up an outdoor grill. It has brought innovation right at our fingertips by bringing all the necessary cooking in a digital one-touch device. It is simple to manage and control. And what makes the Ninja foodi grill apart from other electric grills is the diversity of options it provides for cooking all in a single pot. The ceramic coated interior and accessories make grilling an effortless experience. This cookbook puts the idea of electric grill into perspective by discussing the basics of using the Ninja Foodi Grill. The company has launched the appliance with only one aim that is to provide convenient grilling for all. Try the flavorsome grilling recipes in your Ninja Food grills and experience good taste with amazing aroma, all with little efforts and lesser time. Ninja Foodi Grill offers you with many amazing benefits over outdoor grilling. Let's have a look at what does this modern grilling unit has to offer.

Cyclone Grilling

Being a modern electrical appliance, Ninja Foodi generates high-temperature cyclone heat that circulates the food for even cooking. This cyclone grilling technology cooks differently over the surface and inside the cover of added food. On the outer side, it char-grills while inside it maintains juiciness. That way, you get to enjoy foods that are evenly char-grilled and tender from outside, and soft and juicy from inside.

No Necessary Flipping

Again with outdoor grilling, you have to flip the ingredients in between for even cooking necessarily. While you can quickly flip the parts in Ninja Foodi grill in between, it is not mandatory, though. Ninja Foodi uses cyclone grilling technology that grills inside food evenly without the need to flip.
If a recipe calls for no flipping, then you can grill without any interruption. However, if a recipe calls for flipping in between, open the lid, flip, and continue with cooking. It saves valuable cooking time and offers freedom, as well.

Cook Anytime

You can't grill in your backyard if it's raining heavily or snowing beyond you can tolerate, not to mention stormy weather with high blowing winds. The weather factor is always there to watch out for in outdoor grilling. As you can guess, Ninja Foodi Grill is there for you to cook anytime you crave without worrying about outside weather.

Complete Control
Unlike backyard grilling, Ninja Foodi gives you full control over grilling temperature. In cold weather, you have to adjust the cooking temperature for outdoor grilling. But with indoor automatic grilling, you can grill without keeping in mind outside weather.

You do not need to poke the meat cuts for even cooking as the unit maintains a uniform temperature throughout the cooking process to perfectly caramelize added meat cuts. All you need to do is to add the ingredients, set time, set cooking function, and you are all set.

Compact Design

Not all people have sufficient space and knowledge for backyard grilling. Ninja Foodi is compact in design that takes quite less space in your kitchen. It solves your space issues without making you compromise of quality and taste.

Safe, Easy to Clean, & Economical

Ninja Foodi offers complete cooking safety as it comes with in-build safety features such as auto-shutdown in case of the excessive temperature range. It also provides a completely shock-free cooking experience with a 100% insulated unit. Also, you have to press a few buttons to grill foods, unlike dealing with inflammable fluids and open fires in case of outdoor grilling.

Moreover, this appliance is energy efficient that consumes minimal electricity. It does not add heavily to your electricity bills. Cooking pot, crisping basket, splatter shield, grilling grate, and multi-purpose pan are easy to wash; it saves a lot of post-cooking troubles for you. You can wash them in the dishwasher or wipe them with a clean piece of cloth or a slightly damp piece of fabric.

BREAKFAST

Grilled Bruschetta

Preparation Time: 10 minutes   Cooking Tim e : 8 minutes
Serving: 6

Ingredients :
- 1 cup chopped celery
- 3 tablespoons Dijon mustard
- 1-lb. plum tomatoes, seeded and chopped
- 3 tablespoons balsamic vinegar
- 1/4 cup minced fresh basil
- 3 tablespoons olive oil
- 2 garlic cloves, minced
- 1/2 teaspoon salt

Spread:
- 1 tablespoon finely chopped green onion
- 1/4 cup Dijon mustard
- 1 garlic clove, minced
- 3/4 teaspoon dried oregano
- 1/2 cup mayonnaise
- 1 loaf French bread, sliced

Direction:
1. Take the first eight ingredients in a bowl and mix them together.
2. Cover this prepared topping and refrigerate for about 30 minutes.
3. Now take mayonnaise, onion, garlic, oregano, and mustard in a bowl.
4. Mix them well and prepare the mayonnaise spread.
5. Prepare and preheat the Ninja Foodi Grill in the medium-temperature setting.
6. Once it is preheated, open the lid and place the bread slices on the grill in batches.Cover the Ninja Foodi Grill's lid and let it grill on the "Grilling Mode" for 2 minutes.Flip the bread slices and grill again for 2 minutes.
7. Top the grilled bread with mayonnaise spread and tomato relish.Serve fresh.

Nutrition:
Calories 284 Total Fat 7.9 g Saturated Fat 1.4 g Cholesterol 36 mg Sodium 704 mg Total Carbs 46 g Fiber 3.6 g Sugar 5.5 g Protein 7.9 g

Grilled Chicken Tacos

Preparation Time: 10 minutes   **Cooking Time:** 30 minutes
Serving: 8

Ingredients:
- 2 tablespoons chipotle in adobo sauce, chopped
- 2 teaspoons sugar
- 1/3 cup olive oil
- 1/3 cup lime juice
- 1/3 cup red wine vinegar
- 2 teaspoons salt
- 2 teaspoons pepper
- 1 cup fresh cilantro, chopped
- 2 lbs. boneless skinless chicken thighs
- Taco wraps:
- 8 flour tortillas
- 4 poblano peppers
- 1 tablespoon olive oil
- 2 cups shredded Jack cheese

Direction:
1. Take the first six ingredients in a blender jug and blend them together.
2. Once blended, mix with chipotles and cilantro.
3. Mix chicken with this cilantro marinade and cover to refrigerate for 8 hours.
4. Grease the poblanos with cooking oil and keep them aside.
5. Prepare and preheat the Ninja Foodi Grill on a High-temperature setting.
6. Once it is preheated, open the lid and place the peppers in the grill.
7. Cover the Ninja Foodi Grill's lid and let it grill on the "Grilling Mode" for 2 minutes.
8. Flip the peppers and then continue grilling for another 2 minutes.
9. Its time to grill the chicken in the same grill.
10. Place the chicken in the grill and cover the lid.
11. Select the High-temperature setting on the Grill.
12. Ninja Grill the chicken for 5 minutes per side then transfers to a plate.
13. Now peel and slice the peppers in half then also slice the chicken.
14. Spread each tortilla and add half cup chicken, half peppers and ¼ cup cheese.
15. Fold the tortilla and carefully place in the grill and cover its lid.
16. Grill each for 2 minutes per side on the medium temperature setting.
17. Serve.

Nutrition:
Calories 134 Total Fat 4.7 g Saturated Fat 0.6 g Cholesterol 124mg Sodium 1 mg Total Carbs 54.1 g Fiber 7 g Sugar 3.3 g Protein 26.2 g

Grilled French Toast

Preparation Time: 10 minutes   **Cooking Time:** 8 minutes
Serving: 3

Ingredients:
- 3- 1-inch slices challah bread
- 2 eggs
- Juice of ½ orange
- ½ quart strawberries, quartered
- 1 tablespoon honey
- 1 tablespoon balsamic vinegar
- 1 teaspoon orange zest
- 1/2 sprig fresh rosemary
- ½ teaspoon vanilla extract
- Salt to taste
- 1/4 cup heavy cream
- Fine sugar, for dusting, optional

Direction:
1. Spread a foil sheet on a working surface.
2. Add strawberries, balsamic, orange juice, rosemary, and zest.
3. Fold the foil edges to make a pocket.
4. Whisk egg with cream, honey, vanilla, and a pinch of salt.
5. Dip and soak the bread slices in this mixture and shake off the excess.
6. Prepare and preheat the Ninja Foodi Grill in the medium-temperature setting.
7. Once it is preheated, open the lid and place the bread slices and the foil packet on the grill.
8. Cover the Ninja Foodi Grill's lid and let them grill on the "Grilling Mode" for 2 minutes in batches.
9. Flip the bread slices and continue grilling for another 2 minutes.
10. Serve the bread with the strawberry mix on top.
11. Enjoy.

Nutrition:
Calories 387 Total Fat 6 g Saturated Fat 9.9 g Cholesterol 41 mg Sodium 154 mg Total Carbs 37.4 g Fiber 2.9 g Sugar 15.3 g Protein 14.6 g

Sausage with Eggs

Preparation Time: 10 minutes   **Cooking Time:** 10 minutes
Serving: 4

Ingredients:
- 4 sausage links
- 2 cups chopped kale
- 1 medium sweet yellow onion
- 4 eggs
- 1 cup mushrooms
- olive oil

Direction:
1. Prepare and preheat the Ninja Foodi Grill in a High-temperature setting.
2. Once it is preheated, open the lid and place the sausages on the grill.
3. Cover the Ninja Foodi Grill's lid and let it grill on the "Grilling Mode" for 2 minutes.
4. Flip the sausages and continue grilling for another 3 minutes
5. Now spread the onion, mushrooms, and kale in an iron skillet.
6. Crack the eggs in between the sausages.
7. Bake this mixture for 5 minutes the oven at 350 degrees F.
8. Serve warm and fresh.

Nutrition:
Calories 212 Total Fat 11.8 g Saturated Fat 2.2 g Cholesterol 23mg Sodium 321 mg Total Carbs 14.6 g Dietary Fiber 4.4 g Sugar 8 g Protein 17.3 g

Espresso Glazed Bagels

Preparation Time: 10 minutes   **Cooking Time:** 8 minutes
Serving: 4

Ingredients:
- 4 bagels, split in half
- 1/4 cup coconut milk
- 1 cup fine sugar
- 2 tablespoons black coffee
- 2 tablespoons coconut flakes

Direction:
1. Prepare and preheat the Ninja Foodi Grill on a medium-temperature setting.
2. Once it is preheated, open the lid and place 2 bagels in the grill.

3. Cover the Ninja Foodi Grill's lid and let it grill on the "Grilling Mode" for 2 minutes.
4. Flip the bagel and continue grilling for another 2 minutes.
5. Grill the remaining bagels in a similar way.
6. Whisk the rest of the ingredients in a bowl well.
7. Drizzle this sauce over the grilled bagels.
8. Serve.

Nutrition:
Calories 412 Total Fat 24.8 g Saturated Fat 12.4 g Cholesterol 3 mg Sodium 132 mg Total Carbs 43.8 g Dietary Fiber 3.9 g Sugar 2.5 g Protein 18.9 g

Bruschetta Portobello Mushrooms

Preparation Time: 10 minutes   **Cooking Time:** 8 minutes
Serving: 6

Ingredients:
- 2 cups cherry tomatoes, cut in half
- 3 tablespoons red onion, diced
- 3 tablespoons fresh basil shredded
- Salt and black pepper to taste
- 4 tablespoons butter
- 1 teaspoon dried oregano
- 6 large Portobello Mushrooms, caps only, washed and dried
- For Balsamic glaze:
- 2 teaspoons brown sugar
- 1/4 cup balsamic vinegar

Direction:
1. Start by preparing the balsamic glaze and take all its ingredients in a saucepan.
2. Stir cook this mixture for 8 minutes on medium heat then remove from the heat.
3. Take the mushrooms and brush them with the prepared glaze.
4. Stuff the remaining ingredients into the mushrooms.
5. Prepare and preheat the Ninja Foodi Grill in the medium-temperature setting.
6. Once it is preheated, open the lid and place the stuffed mushrooms in grill with their cap side down.
7. Cover the Ninja Foodi Grill's lid and let it grill on the "Grilling Mode" for 8 minutes.
8. Serve.

Nutrition:
Calories 331 Total Fat 2.5 g Saturated Fat 0.5 g Cholesterol 35 mg Sodium 595 mg Total Carbs 69 g Fiber 12.2 g Sugar 12.5 g Protein 8.7g

Avocado Eggs

Preparation Time: 10 minutes   **Cooking Time:** 5 minutes
Serving: 2

Ingredients:
- 1 ripe avocado
- 1 pinch of barbecue rub
- 2 eggs
- Salt and pepper, to taste
- 1 red jalapeño, finely diced
- 1 tomato, chopped

Direction:
1. Slice the avocado in half and remove its pit.
2. Remove some flesh from the center then crack an egg into the halves.
3. Drizzle barbecue rub, salt, pepper, jalapeno and tomato on top.
4. Prepare and preheat the Ninja Foodi Grill in a High-temperature setting.
5. Once it is preheated, open the lid and place the stuffed avocado in grill with their skin side down.
6. Cover the Ninja Foodi Grill's lid and let it grill on the "Grilling Mode" for 5 minutes.
7. Serve.

Nutrition:
Calories 322 Total Fat 11.8 g Saturated Fat 2.2 g Cholesterol 56 mg Sodium 321 mg Total Carbs 14.6 g Dietary Fiber 4.4 g Sugar 8 g Protein 17.3 g

Coconut French Toast

Preparation Time: 10 minutes   **Cooking Time:** 16 minutes
Serving: 5

Ingredients:
- 1/4 cup milk
- 3 large eggs
- 1 (12-oz. loaf bread- 10 slices
- 1/4 cup sugar
- Cooking spray
- 1 cup of coconut milk
- 10 (1/4-inch-thick slices pineapple, peeled
- 1/2 cup coconut flakes

Direction:
1. Whisk the coconut milk with sugar, eggs, and fat-free milk in a bowl.
2. Dip the bread in this mixture and keep it aside for 1 minute.
3. Prepare and preheat the Ninja Foodi Grill on medium-temperature setting.
4. Once it is preheated, open the lid and place 5 bread slices on the grill.
5. Cover the Ninja Foodi Grill's lid and let it grill on the "Grilling Mode" for 2 minutes.
6. Flip the slices and continue grilling for another 2 minutes.
7. Cook the remaining 5 slices in a similar way.
8. Now grill 5 pineapples slices on the grill for 2 minutes per side.
9. Grill the remaining pineapple in the same way.
10. Serve the bread with pineapple on top.
11. Garnish with coconut and serve.

Nutrition:
Calories 197 Total Fat 15.4 g Saturated Fat 4.2 g Cholesterol 168 mg Sodium 203 mg Total Carbs 58.5 g Sugar 1.1 g Fiber 4 g Protein 7.9 g

Bacon-Herb Grit

Preparation Time: 10 minutes   **Cooking Time:** 10 minutes
Serving: 4

Ingredients:
- 1 tablespoon minced fresh
- 2 teaspoons chopped fresh parsley
- 1/2 teaspoon garlic powder
- 1/2 teaspoon black pepper
- 3 bacon slices, cooked and crumbled
- 1/2 cup shredded cheddar cheese
- 4 cups instant grits
- Cooking spray

Direction:
1. Start by mixing the first seven ingredients in a suitable bowl.
2. Spread this mixture in a 10-inch baking pan and refrigerate for 1 hour.
3. Flip the pan on a plate and cut the grits mixture into 4 triangles.
4. Prepare and preheat the Ninja Foodi Grill in the medium-temperature setting.
5. Once it is preheated, open the lid and place the grit slices in the grill.
6. Cover the Ninja Foodi Grill's lid and let it grill on the "Grilling Mode" for 5 minutes per side.
7. Serve.

Nutrition:
Calories 138 Total Fat 9.7 g Saturated Fat 4.7 g Cholesterol 181 mg Sodium 245 mg Total Carbs 32.5 g Fiber 0.3 g Sugar 1.8 g Protein 10.3 g

Toast Kebabs

Preparation Time: 10 minutes   **Cooking Time:** 6 minutes

Serving: 4

Ingredients:
- 1 loaf (1 lb. bread
- 3/4 cup milk
- 4 large eggs
- 1 teaspoon vanilla extract

Direction:
1. Take all the ingredients in a suitable bowl except the loaf and mix well.
2. Dice the load into even-sized cubes.
3. Dip these cubes in the prepared mixture then thread on the skewers.
4. Prepare and preheat the Ninja Foodi Grill in a low-temperature setting.
5. Once it is preheated, open the lid and place the bread skewers on the grill.
6. Cover the Ninja Foodi Grill's lid and let it grill on the "Grilling Mode" for 2 minutes.
7. Turn the skewers and continue grilling for 2 minutes per side.
8. Serve.

Nutrition:
Calories 391 Total Fat 2.8 g Saturated Fat 0.6 g Cholesterol 330 mg Sodium 62 mg Total Carbs 36.5 g Fiber 9.2 g Sugar 4.5 g Protein 26.6

APPETIZERS & SNACKS

Cob with Pepper Butter

Preparation Time: 10 minutes   **Cooking Time:** 30 minutes

Serving: 8

Ingredients

- 8 medium ears sweet corn
- 1 cup butter, softened
- 2 tablespoons lemon-pepper seasoning

Direction:
1. Season the corn cob with butter and lemon pepper liberally.

2. Prepare and preheat the Ninja Foodi Grill on a medium-temperature setting.
3. Once it is preheated, open the lid and place the corn cob in the grill.
4. Cover the Ninja Foodi Grill's lid and grill on the "Grilling Mode" for 15 minutes while rotating after every 5 minutes.
5. Grill the corn cobs in batches.
6. Serve warm.

Nutrition:
Calories 148 Total Fat 22.4 g Saturated Fat 10.1 g Cholesterol 320 mg Sodium 350 mg Total Carbs 32.2 g Fiber 0.7 g Sugar 0.7 g Protein 4.3 g

Grilled Eggplant

Preparation Time: 10 minutes   **Cooking Time:** 10 minutes
Serving: 4

Ingredients:
- 2 small eggplants, half-inch slices
- 1/4 cup olive oil
- 2 tablespoons lime juice
- 3 teaspoons Cajun seasoning

Direction:
1. Liberally season the eggplant slices with oil, lemon juice, and Cajun seasoning.
2. Prepare and preheat the Ninja Foodi Grill on the medium temperature setting.
3. Once it is preheated, open the lid and place the eggplant slices in the grill.
4. Cover the Ninja Foodi Grill's lid and grill on the "Grilling Mode" for 5 minutes per side.
5. Serve.

Nutrition:
Calories 372 Total Fat 11.1 g Saturated Fat 5.8 g Cholesterol 610 mg Sodium 749 mg Total Carbs 16.9 g Fiber 0.2 g Sugar 0.2 g Protein 13.5 g

Tarragon Asparagus

Preparation Time: 10 minutes   **Cooking Time:** 16 minutes

Serving: 4

Ingredients :
- 2 lbs. fresh asparagus, trimmed
- 2 tablespoons olive oil
- 1 teaspoon salt
- 1/2 teaspoon pepper
- 1/4 cup honey
- 4 tablespoons minced fresh tarragon

Direction:
1. Liberally season the asparagus by tossing with oil, salt, pepper, honey, and tarragon.
2. Prepare and preheat the Ninja Foodi Grill on the medium temperature setting.
3. Once it is preheated, open the lid and place the asparagus on the grill.
4. Cover the Ninja Foodi Grill's lid and grill on the "Grilling Mode" for 8 minutes per side, give them a toss after 4 minutes.
5. Serve warm.

Nutrition:
Calories 248 Total Fat 15.7 g Saturated Fat 2.7 g Cholesterol 75 mg Sodium 94 mg Total Carbs 31.4 g Fiber 0.6 g Sugar 15 g Protein 14.1 g

Grilled Butternut Squash

Preparation Time: 10 minutes   **Cooking Time:** 16 minutes

Serving: 4

Ingredients :
- 1 medium butternut squash
- 1 tablespoon olive oil
- 1 ½ teaspoons dried oregano
- 1 teaspoon dried thyme
- 1/2 teaspoon salt
- 1/4 teaspoon pepper

Direction:
1. Peel and slice the squash into ½ inch thick slices.

2. Remove the center of the slices to discard the seeds.
3. Toss the squash slices with remaining ingredients in a bowl.
4. Prepare and preheat the Ninja Foodi Grill on the medium temperature setting.
5. Once it is preheated, open the lid and place the squash in the grill.
6. Cover the Ninja Foodi Grill's lid and grill on the "Grilling Mode" for 8 minutes per side.
7. Serve warm.

Nutrition:
Calories 249 Total Fat 11.9 g Saturated Fat 1.7 g Cholesterol 78 mg Sodium 79 mg Total Carbs 41.8 g Fiber 1.1 g Sugar 20.3 g Protein 15 g

Honey Glazed Bratwurst

Preparation Time: 10 minutes   **Cooking Time:** 10 minutes
Serving: 4
Ingredients :
- 4 bratwurst links, uncooked
- 1/4 cup Dijon mustard
- 1/4 cup honey
- 2 tablespoons mayonnaise
- 1 teaspoon steak sauce
- 4 brat buns, split

Direction:
1. First, mix the mustard with steak sauce and mayonnaise in a bowl.
2. Prepare and preheat the Ninja Foodi Grill on a High-temperature setting.
3. Once it is preheated, open the lid and place the bratwurst on the grill.
4. Cover the Ninja Foodi Grill's lid and grill on the "Grilling Mode" for 10 minutes per side until their internal temperature reaches 320 degrees F.
5. Serve with buns and mustard sauce on top.

Nutrition:
Calories 213 Total Fat 14 g Saturated Fat 8 g Cholesterol 81 mg Sodium 162 mg Total Carbs 53 g Fiber 0.7 g Sugar 19 g Protein 12 g

Chicken Salad with Blueberry Vinaigrette

Preparation Time: 10 minutes   **Cooking Time:** 14 minutes

Serving: 4

Ingredients :
- 2 boneless skinless chicken breasts, halves
- 1 tablespoon olive oil
- 1 garlic clove, minced
- 1/4 teaspoon salt
- 1/4 teaspoon pepper
- Vinaigrette :
- 1/4 cup olive oil
- 1/4 cup blueberry preserves
- 2 tablespoons balsamic vinegar
- 2 tablespoons maple syrup
- 1/4 teaspoon ground mustard
- 1/8 teaspoon salt
- Dash pepper
- Salads :
- 1 package (10 oz. salad greens
- 1 cup fresh blueberries
- 1/2 cup canned oranges
- 1 cup crumbled goat cheese

Direction:
1. First season the chicken liberally with garlic, salt, pepper and oil in a bowl.
2. Cover to refrigerate for 30 minutes margination.
3. Prepare and preheat the Ninja Foodi Grill on the medium temperature setting.
4. Once it is preheated, open the lid and place the chicken in the grill.
5. Cover the Ninja Foodi Grill's lid and grill on the "Grilling Mode" for 5-7 minutes per side until the internal temperature reaches 330 degrees F.
6. Toss the remaining ingredients for salad and vinaigrette in a bowl.
7. Slice the grilled chicken and serve with salad.

Nutrition:
Calories 379 Total Fat 29.7 g Saturated Fat 18.6 g Cholesterol 141 mg Sodium 193 mg Total Carbs 23.7g Fiber 0.9 g Sugar 19.3 g Protein 5.2 g

Pineapple with Cream Cheese Dip

Preparation Time: 10 minutes   **Cooking Time:** 8 minutes

Serving: 4

Ingredients :
- DIP:
- 3 oz. cream cheese, softened
- 1/4 cup yogurt
- 2 tablespoons honey
- 1 tablespoon brown sugar
- 1 tablespoon lime juice
- 1 teaspoon grated lime zest
- Pineapple:
- 1 fresh pineapple
- 1/4 cup packed brown sugar
- 3 tablespoons honey
- 2 tablespoons lime juice

Direction:
1. First, slice the peeled pineapple into 8 wedges then cut each wedge into 2 spears.
2. Toss the pineapple with sugar, lime juice, and honey in a bowl then refrigerate for 1 hour.
3. Meanwhile, prepare the lime dip by whisking all its ingredients together in a bowl.
4. Remove the pineapple from its marinade.
5. Prepare and preheat the Ninja Foodi Grill on the medium temperature setting.
6. Once it is preheated, open the lid and place the pineapple on the grill.
7. Cover the Ninja Foodi Grill's lid and grill on the "Grilling Mode" for 4 minutes per side.
8. Serve with lime dip.

Nutrition:
Calories 368 Total Fat 6 g Saturated Fat 1.2 g Cholesterol 351 mg Sodium 103 mg Total Carbs 72.8 g Fiber 9.2 g Sugar 32.9 g Protein 7.2 g

Ninja Grill Hot Dogs

Preparation Time: 10 minutes   **Cooking Time:** 12 minutes

Serving: 4

Ingredients :
- 1 cup cabbage slaw
- 4 hot dogs
- 4 bacon slices, crispy
- 4 hot dog buns, cut in half
- 1/8 cup onion, chopped

Direction:
1. Sear the bacon in a skillet until crispy from both the sides.
2. Wrap a bacon strip around each hot dog and secure it by inserting a toothpick.
3. Prepare and preheat the Ninja Foodi Grill in a High-temperature setting.
4. Once it is preheated, open the lid and place 2 hot dogs in the grill.
5. Cover the Ninja Foodi Grill's lid and grill on the "Grilling Mode" for 6 minutes while rotating after every 2 minutes.
6. Cook all the hot dogs in batches then remove the toothpick.
7. Serve warm in a hotdog bun with cabbage slaw and onion.
8. Enjoy.

Nutrition:
Calories 301 Total Fat 32.2 g Saturated Fat 2.4 g Cholesterol 110 mg Sodium 276 mg Total Carbs 25 g Fiber 0.9 g Sugar 31.4 g Protein 28.8 g

VEGETARIAN

Cheddar, Squash And Zucchini Casserole

Preparation Time: 5 minutes   **Cooking Time:** 15 minutes

Serving: 4

Ingredients :
- 1 egg
- 5 saltine crackers, or as needed, crushed
- 2 tablespoons bread crumbs
- 1/2-pound yellow squash, sliced
- 1/2-pound zucchini, sliced
- 1/2 cup shredded Cheddar cheese
- 1-1/2 teaspoons white sugar
- 1/2 teaspoon salt
- 1/4 onion, diced
- 1/4 cup biscuit baking mix
- 1/4 cup butter

Directions:
1. Insert the Crisper Basket, and close the hood. Select AIR CRISP, set the temperature to 360°F, and set the time to 15 minutes. Select START/STOP to begin preheating.
2. Lightly grease baking pan of air fryer with cooking spray. Add onion, zucchini, and yellow squash. Cover pan with foil and for 15 minutes, cook on 360° F or until tender.
3. Stir in salt, sugar, egg, butter, baking mix, and cheddar cheese. Mix well. Fold in crushed crackers. Top with bread crumbs.
4. Air Frying Cook for 15 minutes at 390° F until tops are lightly browned.
5. Serve and enjoy.

Nutrition: Calories 285 Fat 20.5 g Protein 8.6 g

Roasted Vegetables Salad

Preparation Time: 5 minutes   **Cooking Time:** 85 minutes
Serving: 5

Ingredients:
- 3 eggplants
- 1 tbsp of olive oil
- 3 medium zucchini
- 1 tbsp of olive oil
- 4 large tomatoes, cut them in eighths
- 4 cups of one shaped pasta
- 2 peppers of any color
- 1 cup of sliced tomatoes cut into small cubes
- 2 teaspoon of salt substitute
- 8 tbsp of grated parmesan cheese
- ½ cup of Italian dressing
- Leaves of fresh basil

Directions:
1. Wash your eggplant and slice it off then discard the green end. Make sure not to peel. Slice your eggplant into 1/2 inch of thick rounds. 1/2 inch
2. Pour 1 tbsp of olive oil on the eggplant round.
3. Insert the Crisper Basket, and close the hood. Select AIR CRISP, set the temperature to 360°F, and set the time to 40 minutes. Select START/STOP to begin preheating. Air Frying. Put the eggplants in the crisper basket and then toss it in the air fryer. Cook the eggplants for 40 minutes at 360 ° F
4. Meanwhile, wash your zucchini and slice it then discard the green end. But do not peel it. Slice the Zucchini into thick rounds of ½ inch each.
5. In the basket of the Air Fryer, toss your ingredients
6. Add 1 tbsp of olive oil.
7. Air Frying. Cook the zucchini for 25 minutes on a heat of 360° F and when the time is off set it aside. Wash and cut the tomatoes.
8. Air Frying. Arrange your tomatoes in the basket of the air fryer. Set the timer to 30 minutes. Set the heat to 350° F
9. When the time is off, cook your pasta according to the pasta guiding directions, empty it into a colander. Run the cold water on it and wash it and drain the pasta and put it aside. Meanwhile, wash and chop your peppers and place it in a bowl
10. Wash and thinly slice your cherry tomatoes and add it to the bowl. Add your roasted veggies. Add the pasta, a pinch of salt, the topping dressing, add the basil and the parm and toss everything together. (It is better to mix with your hands. Set the ingredients together in the refrigerator, and let it chill Serve your salad and enjoy it!

Zucchini Parmesan Chips

Preparation Time: 10 minutes   Cooking Time: 8 minutes

Serving: 10

Ingredients :
- ½ tsp. paprika
- ½ C. grated parmesan cheese
- ½ C. Italian breadcrumbs
- 1 lightly beaten egg
- 2 thinly sliced zucchinis

Directions:
1. Use a very sharp knife or mandolin slicer to slice zucchini as thinly as you can. Pat off extra moisture.
2. Beat egg with a pinch of pepper and salt and a bit of water.
3. Combine paprika, cheese, and breadcrumbs in a bowl.
4. Dip slices of zucchini into the egg mixture and then into breadcrumb mixture. Press gently to coat.
5. Insert the Crisper Basket, and close the hood. Select AIR CRISP, set the temperature to 350°F, and set the time to 8 minutes. Select START/STOP to begin preheating.
6. Air Frying.
7. With olive oil cooking spray, mist coated zucchini slices. Place into your air fryer in a single layer. Set temperature to 350°F, and set time to 8 minutes.
8. Sprinkle with salt and serve with salsa.

Nutrition:
Calories 211 Fat: 16 g Protein 8 g Sugar 10 g

Zucchini Antipasto

Preparation Time: 5 minutes   **Cooking Time:** 6 minutes

Serving: 4

Ingredients :
- ¼ cup olive oil
- 3 garlic cloves, minced
- 1 tablespoon fresh thyme leaves or ½ teaspoon dried thyme
- ¼ teaspoon salt
- ¼ teaspoon freshly ground black pepper
- 4 medium zucchini, cut lengthwise into ¼-inch-thick slices
- 1 tablespoon balsamic vinegar

Directions :
1. Insert the Grill Grate and close the hood. Select GRILL, set temperature to MAX, and set time to 8 minutes. Select START/STOP to begin preheating.
2. Whisk together the olive oil, garlic, thyme, salt, and pepper in a large bowl. Add the zucchini and toss to coat. Grill for about 6 minutes, until the zucchini slices have taken on grill marks and are very tender.
3. Serve either hot off the grill or at room temperature, sprinkled with the vinegar.

Nutrition: Calories 156   Fat 14 g   Protein 2 g

Jalapeño Cheese Balls

Preparation Time: 10 minutes   **Cooking Time:** 12 minutes

Serving: 12

Ingredients :
- 4 ounces cream cheese
- ⅓ cup shredded mozzarella cheese
- ⅓ cup shredded Cheddar cheese
- 2 jalapeños, finely chopped
- ½ cup bread crumbs
- 2 eggs
- ½ cup all-purpose flour
- Salt
- Pepper
- Cooking oil

Directions:
1. In a medium bowl, combine the cream cheese, mozzarella, Cheddar, and jalapeños. Mix well.
2. Form the cheese mixture into balls about an inch thick. Using a small ice cream scoop works well.
3. Arrange the cheese balls on a sheet pan and place in the freezer for 15 minutes. This will help the cheese balls maintain their shape while frying.

4. Insert the Crisper Basket, and close the hood. Select AIR CRISP, set the temperature to 350°F, and set the time to 12 minutes. Select START/STOP to begin preheating.
5. Spray the crisper basket with cooking oil. Place the bread crumbs in a small bowl. In another small bowl, beat the eggs. In a third small bowl, combine the flour with salt and pepper to taste, and mix well. Remove the cheese balls from the freezer. Dip the cheese balls in the flour, then the eggs, and then the bread crumbs.
6. Air Frying. Place the cheese balls in the air fryer. Spray with cooking oil. Cook for 8 minutes.
7. Open the air fryer and flip the cheese balls. I recommend flipping them instead of shaking so the balls maintain their form. Cook an additional 4 minutes. Cool before serving.

Nutrition: Calories 96 Fat 6 g Protein 4 g Sugar 5 g

Jicama Fries

Preparation Time: 10 minutes   **Cooking Tim e :** 5 minutes
Serving: 8

Ingredients :
- 1 tbsp. dried thyme
- ¾ C. arrowroot flour
- ½ large Jicama
- eggs

Directions:
1. Sliced jicama into fries.
2. Whisk eggs together and pour over fries. Toss to coat.
3. Mix a pinch of salt, thyme, and arrowroot flour together. Toss egg-coated jicama into dry mixture, tossing to coat well.
4. Insert the Crisper Basket, and close the hood. Select AIR CRISP, set the temperature to 350°F, and set the time to 5 minutes. Select START/STOP to begin preheating.
5. Air frying. Spray the air fryer basket with olive oil and add fries. Cook at 350°F, for 5 minutes. Toss halfway into the cooking process.

Nutrition: Calories 211 Fat 19 g Protein 9 g Sugar 1 g

Sage And Garlic Grilled Tomatoes

Preparation Time: 5 minutes   **Cooking Time:** 6 minutes

Serving: 6

Ingredients :
- 6 plum tomatoes (about 1¼ pounds, cut in half lengthwise
- 2 tablespoons extra-virgin olive oil
- Coarse salt (kosher or sea and cracked black pepper
- 3 cloves garlic, minced
- 1 tablespoon finely chopped fresh sage, plus 12 whole fresh sage leaves

Directions :
1. Brush the tomato halves all over with olive oil. Season them generously all over with salt and pepper, then sprinkle the garlic and chopped sage over them. Press a whole sage leaf in the center of the cut side of each tomato half. Set any leftover olive oil aside.
2. Insert the Grill Grate and close the hood. Select GRILL, set temperature to MAX, and set time to 8 minutes. Select START/STOP to begin preheating.
3. Arrange the tomato halves on the hot grill, cut side up, then close the hood. The tomatoes will be done after cooking 4 to 6 minutes until nicely browned.
4. Transfer the tomatoes to a platter or plates and drizzle any remaining olive oil over them. Serve at once.

Nutrition:
Calories 145   Fat 11 g   Protein 3 g   Sugar 2 g

Crispy Roasted Broccoli

Preparation Time: 10 minutes   **Cooking Time:** 10 minutes

Serving: 2

Ingredients :
- ¼ tsp. Masala
- ½ tsp. red chili powder
- ½ tsp. salt
- ¼ tsp. turmeric powder
- 1 tbsp. chickpea flour
- 2 tbsp. yogurt
- 1 pound broccoli

Directions:
1. Cut broccoli up into florets. Soak in a bowl of water with 2 teaspoons of salt for at least half an hour to remove impurities.
2. Take out broccoli florets from water and let drain. Wipe down thoroughly.
3. Mix all other ingredients together to create a marinade.
4. Toss broccoli florets in the marinade. Cover and chill 15-30 minutes.
5. Insert the Crisper Basket, and close the hood. Select AIR CRISP, set the temperature to 390°F, and set the time to 10 minutes. Select START/STOP to begin preheating.
6. Air frying. Place marinated broccoli florets into the fryer, cook 350°F, for 10 minutes. Florets will be crispy when done.

Nutrition:
Calories 96   Fat 2 g   Protein 7 g   Sugar 5 g

Creamy And Cheese Broccoli Bake

Preparation Time: 5 minutes   **Cooking Time:** 20 minutes

Serving: 2

Ingredients :
- 1 pound fresh broccoli, coarsely chopped
- 2 tablespoons all-purpose flour
- salt to taste
- 1 tablespoon dry bread crumbs, or to taste
- 1/2 large onion, coarsely chopped
- 1/2 (14 ounce can evaporated milk, divided
- 1/2 cup cubed sharp Cheddar cheese
- 1-1/2 teaspoons butter, or to taste
- 1/4 cup water

Directions:
1. Lightly grease baking pan with cooking spray. Mix in half of the milk and flour in pan and for 5 minutes, cook on 360°F. Halfway through cooking time, mix well. Add broccoli and remaining milk. Mix well and cook for another 5 minutes.
2. Stir in cheese and mix well until melted.
3. In a small bowl mix well, butter and bread crumbs. Sprinkle on top of broccoli.
4. Cook for 20 minutes at 360°F until tops are lightly browned.
5. Serve and enjoy.

Nutrition:
Calories 444   Fat 22 g   Protein 23 g

Grilled Artichokes with Honey Dijon

Preparation Time: 5 minutes   **Cooking Time:** 15 minutes
Serving: 6

Ingredients :
- 6 whole artichokes
- ½ gallon water
- 3 Tbsp. sea salt
- olive oil
- sea salt to taste
- ¼ cup raw honey
- ¼ cup boiling water
- 3 Tbsp. Dijon mustard

Directions :
1. Cut the artichokes in half lengthwise top to bottom.
2. Mix the 3 tablespoons of sea salt and water together. Place the artichokes in the brine for 30 minutes to several hours before cooking.
3. Insert the Grill Grate and close the hood. Select GRILL, set temperature to MAX, and set time to 8 minutes. Select START/STOP to begin preheating.
4. Remove the artichokes from the brine, drizzle with olive oil on the cut side, and season with sea salt.
5. Grill for 15 minutes on each side, cut side down first.
6. Turn the grill down to low, and turn the artichokes cut-side down while you mix the honey, boiling water, and Dijon.
7. Turn the artichokes back over, and brush the Dijon mix well over the cut side until it is all absorbed.
8. Serve alongside a protein like salmon, beef, pork, or chicken, or with rice or potatoes for a vegetarian option.

Coconut Battered Cauliflower Bites

Preparation Time: 5 minutes   **Cooking Time:** 20 minutes

Serves: 4

Ingredients :
- salt and pepper to taste
- 1 flax egg (1 tablespoon flaxseed meal + 3 tablespoon water
- 1 small cauliflower, cut into florets
- 1 teaspoon mixed spice
- ½ teaspoon mustard powder
- 2 tablespoons maple syrup
- 1 clove of garlic, minced
- 2 tablespoons soy sauce
- 1/3 cup oats flour
- 1/3 cup plain flour
- 1/3 cup desiccated coconut

Directions:
1. Insert the Crisper Basket, and close the hood. Select AIR CRISP, set the temperature to 400°F, and set the time to 15 minutes. Select START/STOP to begin preheating.
2. In a mixing bowl, mix together oats, flour, and desiccated coconut. Season with salt and pepper to taste. Set aside.
3. In another bowl, place the flax egg and add a pinch of salt to taste. Set aside.
4. Season the cauliflower with mixed spice and mustard powder.
5. Dredge the florets in the flax egg first then in the flour mixture.
6. Air frying. Place inside the air fryer and cook for 15 minutes.
7. Meanwhile, place the maple syrup, garlic, and soy sauce in a sauce pan and heat over medium flame. Bring to a boil and adjust the heat to low until the sauce thickens.
8. After 15 minutes, take out the florets from the air fryer and place them in the saucepan.
9. Toss to coat the florets and place inside the air fryer and cook for another 5 minutes.

Nutrition:
Calories 154   Fat 3 g   Protein 5 g

Grilled Eggplant With Feta And Lemon

Preparation Time: 5 minutes   **Cooking Time:** 15 minutes

Serving: 4

Ingredients :
- 1 large eggplant, cut into ½-inch slices
- 1 tablespoon salt
- 3 tablespoons olive oil
- 4 ounces feta cheese, crumbled
- ½ teaspoon sweet paprika
- Freshly ground black pepper
- 1 lemon, cut in half

Directions :
1. Spread the eggplant slices on a rimmed baking sheet and sprinkle with half of the salt. Flip the slices and sprinkle with the remaining salt. Let sit for 15 minutes to take away some of the bitterness of the eggplant. Transfer the slices to sheets of paper towels and pat dry.
2. Insert the Grill Grate and close the hood. Select GRILL, set temperature to MAX, and set time to 8 minutes. Select START/STOP to begin preheating.
3. Brush both sides of the eggplant slices with the olive oil. Grill for about 6 minutes, until the slices have taken on grill marks and are golden brown.
4. Transfer the eggplant to a serving platter and top with the feta, paprika, some pepper, and a squirt of lemon juice. Serve hot or at room temperature. 4

Nutrition:
Calories 204   Fat 17 g   Protein 6 g

Crispy Jalapeno Coins

Preparation Time: 10 minutes   **Cooking Time:** 5 minutes

Serving: 2

Ingredients :
- 1 egg
- 2-3 tbsp. coconut flour
- 1 sliced and seeded jalapeno
- Pinch of garlic powder
- Pinch of onion powder
- Pinch of Cajun seasoning (optional
- Pinch of pepper and salt

Directions:
1. Insert the Crisper Basket, and close the hood. Select AIR CRISP, set the temperature to 400°F, and set the time to 5 minutes. Select START/STOP to begin preheating.
2. Mix together all dry ingredients.
3. Pat jalapeno slices dry. Dip coins into egg wash and then into dry mixture. Toss to thoroughly coat.
4. Add coated jalapeno slices to air fryer in a singular layer. Spray with olive oil.
5. Air frying. Cook at 350°F, for 5 minutes. Cook just till crispy.

Nutrition: Calories 128   Fat 8 g   Protein 7 g

Grilled Brussels Sprouts with Balsamic Glaze

Preparation Time: 5 minutes   **Cooking Time:** 10 minutes

Serving: 4

Ingredients :
- brussels sprouts
- olive oil
- sea salt to taste
- balsamic vinegar

Directions :
1. Cut the sprouts in half lengthwise from top to bottom.
2. Brush with olive oil and season with sea salt.
3. Insert the Grill Grate and close the hood. Select GRILL, set temperature to MAX, and set time to 8 minutes. Select START/STOP to begin preheating.
4. Grill the sprouts cut-side down for 5 minutes on each side.
5. Brush the sprouts lightly with balsamic, and grill for a minute or so more to set the vinegar before serving.

Spaghetti Squash Tots

Preparation Time: 10 minutes   **Cooking Time:** 15 minutes

Serving: 8

Ingredients :
- ¼ tsp. pepper
- ½ tsp. salt
- 1 thinly sliced scallion
- 1 spaghetti squash

Directions:
1. Wash and cut the squash in half lengthwise. Scrape out the seeds.
2. With a fork, remove spaghetti meat by strands and throw out skins.
3. In a clean towel, toss in squash and wring out as much moisture as possible. Place in a bowl and with a knife slice through meat a few times to cut up smaller.
4. Add pepper, salt, and scallions to squash and mix well.
5. Insert the Crisper Basket, and close the hood. Select AIR CRISP, set the temperature to 350°F, and set the time to 15 minutes. Select START/STOP to begin preheating.
6. Air frying. Create "tot" shapes with your hands and place in the air fryer. Spray with olive oil. Cook at 350°F, for 15 minutes. Cook until golden and crispy!

Nutritoin: Calories 231   Fat 18 g   Protein 5 g

Buffalo Cauliflower

Preparation Time: 5 minutes   **Cooking Time:** 15 minutes

Serving: 4

Ingredients :
- Cauliflower:
- 1 C. panko breadcrumbs
- 1 tsp. salt
- 4 C. cauliflower florets
- Buffalo Coating:
- ¼ C. Vegan Buffalo sauce
- ¼ C. melted vegan butter

Directions:
1. Melt butter in microwave and whisk in buffalo sauce.
2. Dip each cauliflower floret into buffalo mixture, ensuring it gets coated well. Hold over a bowl till floret is done dripping.
3. Mix breadcrumbs with salt.

4. Insert the Crisper Basket, and close the hood. Select AIR CRISP, set the temperature to 350°F, and set the time to 15 minutes. Select START/STOP to begin preheating.
5. Air frying. Dredge dipped florets into breadcrumbs and place into air fryer. Cook at 350°F, for 15 minutes. When slightly browned, they are ready to eat.
6. Serve with your favorite keto dipping sauce.

Crisped Baked Cheese Stuffed Chile Pepper

Preparation Time: 10 minutes   Cooking Tim e : 30 minutes
Serving: 3
Ingredients :
- 1 (7) ounce can whole green Chile peppers, drained
- 1 egg, beaten
- 1 tablespoon all-purpose flour
- 1/2 (5 ounce can evaporated milk
- 1/2 (8 ounce can tomato sauce
- 1/4-pound Monterey Jack cheese, shredded
- 1/4-pound Longhorn or Cheddar cheese, shredded
- 1/4 cup milk

Directions:
1. Lightly grease baking pan with cooking spray. Evenly spread chilies and sprinkle cheddar and Jack cheese on top.
2. In a bowl whisk well flour, milk, and eggs. Pour over chilies.
3. For 20 minutes, cook on 360°F
4. Add tomato sauce on top.
5. Cook for 10 minutes at 390°F until tops are lightly browned.
6. Serve and enjoy.

Nutrition: Calories 392   Fat 28 g   Protein 24 g

Jumbo Stuffed Mushrooms

Preparation Time: 10 minutes   **Cooking Time:** 9 minutes

Serving: 4

Ingredients :
- 4 jumbo portobello mushrooms
- 1 tablespoon olive oil
- ¼ cup ricotta cheese
- 5 tablespoons Parmesan cheese, divided
- 1 cup frozen chopped spinach, thawed and drained
- ⅓ cup bread crumbs
- ¼ teaspoon minced fresh rosemary

Directions:
1. Wipe the mushrooms with a damp cloth. Remove the stems and discard. Using a spoon, gently scrape out most of the gills.
2. Rub the mushrooms with the olive oil.
3. Insert the Crisper Basket, and close the hood. Select AIR CRISP, set the temperature to 350°F, and set the time to 3 minutes. Select START/STOP to begin preheating.
4. Air frying Put in the crisper basket, hollow side up, and bake for 3 minutes. Carefully remove the mushroom caps, because they will contain liquid. Drain the liquid out of the caps.
5. In a medium bowl, combine the ricotta, 3 tablespoons of Parmesan cheese, spinach, bread crumbs, and rosemary, and mix well.
6. Stuff this mixture into the drained mushroom caps. Sprinkle with the remaining 2 tablespoons of Parmesan cheese.
7. Put the mushroom caps back into the basket and bake for 4 to 6 minutes or until the filling is hot and the mushroom caps are tender.

Nutrition:
Calories 117   Fat 7 g   Protein 7 g   Fiber 2 g

Crispy And Healthy Avocado Fingers

Preparation Time: 10 minutes   **Cooking Time:** 10 minutes

Serving: 4

Ingredients :
- ½ cup panko breadcrumbs
- ½ teaspoon salt
- 1 pitted Haas avocado, peeled and sliced
- liquid from 1 can white beans or aquafaba

Directions:
1. Insert the Crisper Basket, and close the hood. Select AIR CRISP, set the temperature to 350°F, and set the time to 8 minutes. Select START/STOP to begin preheating.
2. In a shallow bowl, toss the breadcrumbs and salt until well combined.
3. Dredge the avocado slices first with the aquafaba then in the breadcrumb mixture.
4. Place the avocado slices in a single layer inside the crisper basket.
5. Air frying. Cook for 10 minutes and shake halfway through the cooking time.

Nutrition : Calories 51   Fat 8 g   Protein 2 g

Cinnamon Butternut Squash Fries

Preparation Time: 5 minutes   **Cooking Time:** 10 minutes

Serving: 6

Ingredients :
- 1 pinch of salt
- ½ tsp. nutmeg
- 2 tsp. cinnamon
- 10 ounces pre-cut butternut squash fries
- 1 tbsp. powdered unprocessed sugar
- 1 tbsp. coconut oil

Directions:
1. In a plastic bag, pour in all ingredients. Coat fries with other components till coated and sugar is dissolved.
2. Insert the Crisper Basket, and close the hood. Select AIR CRISP, set the temperature to 390°F, and set the time to 10 minutes. Select START/STOP to begin preheating.
3. Air frying. Spread coated fries into a single layer in the air fryer. Cook at 390°F for 10 minutes. Cook until crispy.

Nutrition: Calories 175   Fat 8 g   Protein 1 g

FISH AND SEAFOOD

Spanish Shrimp

Preparation Time: 5 minutes   Cooking Time : 3 minutes
Serving: 4

Ingredients :
- 1½ pounds shelled and deveined medium shrimp
- ½ cup olive oil
- 2 garlic cloves, minced
- ½ teaspoon salt
- ½ teaspoon red pepper flakes
- 1 lemon, cut into wedges

Directions :
1. Rinse the shrimp and pat dry with paper towels. Combine the shrimp, olive oil, garlic, salt, and red pepper flakes in a medium bowl. Toss gently to combine. Cover with plastic wrap and then refrigerate for at least 30 minutes or up to 2 hours.
2. Insert the Grill Grate and close the hood. Select GRILL, set temperature to HIGH, and set time to 8 minutes. Select START/STOP to begin preheating.
3. Grill the shrimp for about 3 minutes, until they are opaque and firm to the touch. Serve the shrimp immediately in 4 small bowls with the lemon wedges.

Nutrition:
Calories 305   Fat 17 g   Protein 35 g

Healthy Fish and Chips

Preparation Time: 5 minutes   Cooking Tim e : 15 minutes
Serving: 3

Ingredients :
- Old Bay seasoning
- ½ C. panko breadcrumbs
- 1 egg
- 2 tbsp. almond flour
- 4-6 ounce tilapia fillets
- Frozen crinkle cut fries

Directions:
1. Add almond flour to one bowl, beat egg in another bowl, and add panko breadcrumbs to the third bowl, mixed with Old Bay seasoning.
2. Dredge tilapia in flour, then egg, and then breadcrumbs.
3. Insert the Crisper Basket, and close the hood. Select AIR CRISP, set the temperature to 390°F, and set the time to 15 minutes. Select START/STOP to begin preheating. Place coated fish in the crisper basket along with fries.
4. Air frying. Cook at 390°F for 15 minutes.

Nutrition:
Calories 219   Fat 5 g   Protein 25 g   Sugar 1 g

Moroccan Salmon

Preparation Time: 5 minutes   Cooking Tim e : 5 minutes
Serving: 4

Ingredients :
- ½ cup fresh cilantro leaves
- ½ cup fresh flat-leaf parsley leaves
- 2 cloves garlic, coarsely chopped
- 1 teaspoon sweet paprika
- ½ teaspoon coarse salt (kosher or sea, or more to taste
- ½ teaspoon freshly ground black pepper
- ½ teaspoon ground coriander
- ½ teaspoon ground cumin
- ½ teaspoon hot red pepper flakes, or more to taste
- 3 tablespoons fresh lemon juice, or more to taste
- ½ cup extra-virgin olive oil
- 4 pieces salmon fillet or salmon steaks (each 6 to 8 ounces)

Directions :
1. Place the cilantro, parsley, garlic, paprika, salt, black pepper, coriander, cumin, and hot pepper flakes in a food processor and pulse the machine to finely chop. Add the lemon juice and process until a coarse purée forms. With the motor running, add the olive oil in a thin stream. Taste for seasoning, adding more salt, hot pepper flakes, and/or lemon juice as necessary; the charmoula should be highly seasoned.
2. If using salmon fillets, run your fingers over them, feeling for bones. Using needle-nose pliers or tweezers, pull out any you find (you will not need to do this with salmon steaks. Rinse the fish under cold running water, then blot it dry with paper towels. Pour a third of the charmoula over the bottom of a nonreactive baking dish just large enough to hold the salmon in one layer. Arrange the salmon pieces on top. Spoon half of the remaining charmoula over the fish, then set the rest of the charmoula aside. Let the salmon marinate in the refrigerator, covered, for 2 to 4 hours (the longer it marinates, the richer the flavor will be.
3. When ready to cook, drain the salmon and discard the marinade. Insert the Grill Grate and close the hood. Select GRILL, set temperature to HIGH, and set time to 8 minutes. Select START/STOP to begin preheating.
4. Place the salmon on the hot grill grate, then close the lid. The salmon will be done after cooking 3 to 5 minutes until it is browned and cooked through. To test for doneness, press the fish with your finger; it should break into clean flakes.Arrange the salmon on a platter or plates. Stir the remaining charmoula to recombine, then spoon it on top of the salmon.

Quick Paella

Preparation Time: 7 minutes   **Cooking Time:** 15 minutes
Serving: 4

Ingredients:
- 1 -10-ounce package frozen cooked rice, thawed
- 1 -6-ounce jar artichoke hearts, drained and chopped
- ¼ cup vegetable broth
- ½ teaspoon turmeric
- ½ teaspoon dried thyme
- 1 cup frozen cooked small shrimp
- ½ cup frozen baby peas
- 1 tomato, diced

Directions:
1. In a 6-by-6-by-2-inch pan, combine the rice, artichoke hearts, vegetable broth, turmeric, and thyme, and stir gently. Insert the Crisper Basket, and close the hood. Select AIR CRISP, set the temperature to 390°F, and set the time to 10 minutes. Select START/STOP to begin preheating
2. Air frying. Place in the crisper basket and bake for 8 to 9 minutes or until the rice is hot. Remove from the air fryer and gently stir in the shrimp, peas, and tomato. Cook for 5 to 8 minutes or until the shrimp and peas are hot and the paella is bubbling.

Nutrition:

Calories 345   Fat 1 g   Protein 18 g   Fiber 4 g

Grilled Teriyaki-Glazed Coho Salmon

Preparation Time: 5 minutes   **Cooking Time:** 25 minutes
Serving: 2

Ingredients :
- 1–2 coho salmon filets
- SAUCE
- 1 cup water
- ¼ cup brown sugar
- ¼ cup soy sauce
- 1 Tbsp. honey
- 1½ Tbsp. finely minced ginger root (about 1-inch piece
- 2 cloves garlic, finely minced
- ½ tsp. white pepper
- THICKENER
- 2 Tbsp. cornstarch
- ¼ cup cold water

Directions :
1. Insert the Grill Grate and close the hood. Select GRILL, set temperature to HIGH, and set time to 15 minutes. Select START/STOP to begin preheating.
2. In medium saucepan over medium heat, combine sauce ingredients and bring to a low boil.
3. Once sauce reaches a low boil, use a fork and mix together cornstarch and water in separate bowl until thoroughly incorporated. Slowly whisk cornstarch mixture into sauce until it thickens.
4. Add one chunk of pecan wood to the hot coals of your grill
5. Brush sauce onto salmon filets, Place on the hot grill grate, then close the hood, and cook for 15 minutes.
6. Brush salmon with another coat of sauce, close lid, and cook for an additional 10 minutes.
7. Remove from grill, garnish, and serve hot.

Cilantro-Lime Fried Shrimp

Preparation Time: 10 minutes   Cooking Time: 8 minutes

Serving: 4

Ingredients :

- 1 pound raw shrimp, peeled and deveined with tails on or off (see Prep tip
- ½ cup chopped fresh cilantro
- Juice of 1 lime
- 1 egg
- ½ cup all-purpose flour
- ¾ cup bread crumbs
- Salt
- Pepper
- Cooking oil
- ½ cup cocktail sauce (optional)

Directions:

1. Place the shrimp in a plastic bag and add the cilantro and lime juice. Seal the bag. Shake to combine. Marinate in the refrigerator for 30 minutes.
2. Insert the Crisper Basket, and close the hood. Select AIR CRISP, set the temperature to 390°F, and set the time to 10 minutes. Select START/STOP to begin preheating.
3. In a small bowl, beat the egg. In another small bowl, place the flour. Place the bread crumbs in a third small bowl, and season with salt and pepper to taste.
4. Spray the crisper basket with cooking oil.
5. Remove the shrimp from the plastic bag. Dip each in the flour, then the egg, and then the bread crumbs.
6. Air Frying.
7. Place the shrimp in the crisper basket. It is okay to stack them. Spray the shrimp with cooking oil. Cook for 4 minutes.
8. Open the air fryer and flip the shrimp. I recommend flipping individually instead of shaking to keep the breading intact. Cook for an additional 4 minutes, or until crisp.
9. Cool before serving. Serve with cocktail sauce if desired.

Nutrition:

Calories 254   Fat 4 g   Protein 29 g   Fiber 1 g

Halibut

Preparation Time: 5 minutes   **Cooking Time:** 4 minutes
Serving: 4
Ingredients

- halibut fillets, cut about 1 inch thick
- olive oil
- sea salt and pepper
- fresh grated parmesan cheese
- fresh chopped parsley
- fresh lemon juice

Directions:

1. Brush the halibut fillets with the olive oil and sprinkle with the salt and pepper.
2. Insert the Grill Grate and close the hood. Select GRILL, set temperature to HIGH, and set time to 8 minutes. Select START/STOP to begin preheating.
3. Place the halibut on the hot grill grate, then close the hood, and Grill for 4 minutes.
4. Turn the grill down to medium, and grill for 4 minutes more.
5. Sprinkle the halibut with the parmesan, and grill an additional minute before removing from the heat.
6. Sprinkle the fillets with parsley and lemon juice, and let it relax for 5 minutes before serving.

Lemony Tuna

Preparation Time: 10 minutes   Cooking Tim e : 10 minutes
Serving: 4

Ingredients:
- 2 (6-ounce cans water packed plain tuna
- 2 teaspoons Dijon mustard
- ½ cup breadcrumbs
- 1 tablespoon fresh lime juice
- 2 tablespoons fresh parsley, chopped
- 1 egg
- air fryer of hot sauce
- 3 tablespoons canola oil
- Salt and freshly ground black pepper, to taste

Directions:

1. Drain most of the liquid from the canned tuna.
2. In a bowl, add the fish, mustard, crumbs, citrus juice, parsley and hot sauce and mix till well combined. Add a little canola oil if it seems too dry. Add egg, salt and stir to combine. Make the patties from tuna mixture. Refrigerate the tuna patties for about 2 hours.
3. Insert the Crisper Basket, and close the hood. Select AIR CRISP, set the temperature to 355°F, and set the time to 10 minutes. Select START/STOP to begin preheating.
4. Air frying. Cook for about 10-12 minutes

Grilled Soy Salmon Fillets

Preparation Time: 5 minutes   Cooking Tim e : 8 minutes
Serving: 4

Ingredients :
- 4 salmon fillets
- 1/4 teaspoon ground black pepper
- 1/2 teaspoon cayenne pepper
- 1/2 teaspoon salt
- 1 teaspoon onion powder
- 1 tablespoon fresh lemon juice
- 1/2 cup soy sauce
- 1/2 cup water
- 1 tablespoon honey
- 2 tablespoons extra-virgin olive oil

Directions:
1. Firstly, pat the salmon fillets dry using kitchen towels. Season the salmon with black pepper, cayenne pepper, salt, and onion powder.
2. To make the marinade, combine together the lemon juice, soy sauce, water, honey, and olive oil. Marinate the salmon for at least 2 hours in your refrigerator.
3. Insert the Grill Grate and close the hood. Select GRILL, set temperature to HIGH, and set time to 8 minutes. Select START/STOP to begin preheating.
4. Arrange the fish fillets on the grill grate.
5. Grill at 330 degrees for 8 to 9 minutes, or until salmon fillets are easily flaked with a fork.
6. Work with batches and serve warm.

Simple Grilled Swordfish

Preparation Time: 5 minutes   **Cooking Time:** 4 minutes

Serving: 4

Ingredients :
- 4 (6-ounce swordfish steaks, about I inch thick
- ¼ cup olive oil
- Juice of ½ lemon
- ½ teaspoon dried oregano
- ½ teaspoon salt
- ¼ teaspoon freshly ground black pepper

Directions :

1. Rinse the fish and pat dry with paper towels.
2. Combine the olive oil, lemon juice, and oregano in a shallow baking dish large enough to fit all the swordfish steaks. Add the swordfish steaks and marinate for about 15 minutes. Turn the steaks and marinate for another 15 minutes.
3. Insert the Grill Grate and close the hood. Select GRILL, set temperature to HIGH, and set time to 8 minutes. Select START/STOP to begin preheating.
4. Sprinkle the swordfish steaks with the salt and pepper. Grill for about 4 minutes. To test for doneness, prod an edge of the swordfish with a fork. The fish should flake easily. Serve immediately.

Nutrition:

Calories 327 Fat 21 g   Protein 34 g

Flying Fish

Preparation Time: 5 minutes   Cooking Tim e : 12 minutes
Serving: 6

Ingredients :
- 4 Tbsp Oil
- 3-4 oz Breadcrumbs
- 1 Whisked Whole Egg in a Saucer/Soup Plate
- 4 Fresh Fish Fillets
- Fresh Lemon (For serving)

Directions:

1. Insert the Crisper Basket, and close the hood. Select AIR CRISP, set the temperature to 350°F, and set the time to 12 minutes. Select START/STOP to begin preheating.
2. Mix the crumbs and oil until it looks nice and loose.
3. Dip the fish in the egg and coat lightly, then move on to the crumbs. Make sure the fillet is covered evenly.
4. Air Frying.
5. Cook in the crisper basket for roughly 12 minutes – depending on the size of the fillets you are using.
6. Serve with fresh lemon & chips to complete the duo.

"Barbecued" Salmon

Preparation Time: 5 minutes   Cooking Time : 5 minutes
Serving: 4
Ingredients :
- 4 pieces skinless salmon fillet (each about 6 ounces
- 2 tablespoons Basic Barbecue Rub
- 2 tablespoons olive oil
- 1 teaspoon liquid smoke
- BARBECUE VINAIGRETTE
- 1 tablespoon red barbecue sauce
- 1 tablespoon fresh lemon juice
- 3 tablespoons olive oil
- 1 tablespoon very finely diced sweet onion
- 1 tablespoon very finely diced seeded tomato
- 1 tablespoon very finely diced green bell pepper
- Coarse salt (kosher or sea and freshly ground black pepper

Directions :

1. Run your fingers over the fish fillets, feeling for bones. Using needle-nose pliers or tweezers, pull out any you find. Rinse the fish under cold running water, then blot it dry with paper towels. Sprinkle the barbecue rub all over the fish, patting it on with your fingertips. Let the fish cure at room temperature for 10 minutes.
2. Place the olive oil and liquid smoke in a small bowl and stir with a fork. Set the basting mixture aside.Insert the Grill Grate and close the hood. Select GRILL, set temperature to HIGH, and set time to 8 minutes. Select START/STOP to begin preheating.
3. Place the fish on the hot grill grate, then close the hood. The fish will be cooked through after 3 to 5 minutes (if you prefer it pink in the center, cook it a minute or so less. You will need to turn the fish so that you can baste both sides until it is just cooked through. To test for doneness, press the fish with your finger; it should break into clean flakes. Start basting the fish with the olive oil mixture after 1 minute and baste both sides at least twice.
4. Transfer the fish to a platter or plates. Spoon the Barbecue Vinaigrette on top, if using, and serve at once.BARBECUE VINAIGRETTE
5. Place the barbecue sauce in a small nonreactive bowl. Gradually whisk in 2 tablespoons of water and the lemon juice, olive oil, onion, tomato, and bell pepper. Season with salt and pepper to taste. The sauce is best made no more than an hour before serving.

Pistachio-Crusted Lemon-Garlic Salmon

Preparation Time: 5 minutes   **Cooking Time:** 20 minutes

Serving: 6

Ingredients :
- 4 medium-sized salmon filets
- 2 raw eggs
- 3 ounces of melted butter
- 1 clove of garlic, peeled and finely minced
- 1 large-sized lemon
- 1 teaspoon of salt
- 1 tablespoon of parsley, rinsed, patted dry and chopped
- 1 teaspoon of dill, rinsed, patted dry and chopped
- ½ cup of pistachio nuts, shelled and coarsely crushed

Directions:

1. Cover the crisper basket with a lining of tin foil, leaving the edges uncovered to allow air to circulate through the basket.
2. Insert the Crisper Basket, and close the hood. Select AIR CRISP, set the temperature to 350°F, and set the time to 10 minutes. Select START/STOP to begin preheating.
3. In a mixing bowl, beat the eggs until fluffy and until the yolks and whites are fully combined.
4. Add the melted butter, the juice of the lemon, the minced garlic, the parsley and the dill to the beaten eggs, and stir thoroughly.
5. One by one, dunk the salmon filets into the wet mixture, then roll them in the crushed pistachios, coating completely.
6. Place the coated salmon fillets in the crisper basket.
7. Air Frying.
8. When the air fryer shuts off, after 10 minutes, the salmon will be partly cooked and the crust beginning to crisp. Using tongs, turn each of the fish filets over.
9. Reset the air fryer to 350 degrees for another 10 minutes.
10. After 10 minutes, when the air fryer shuts off, the salmon will be perfectly cooked and the pistachio crust will be toasted and crispy. Using tongs, remove from the air fryer and serve.

Louisiana Shrimp Po Boy

Preparation Time: 10 minutes   **Cooking Time:** 10 minutes

Serving: 6

Ingredients :
- 1 tsp. creole seasoning
- 8 slices of tomato
- Lettuce leaves
- ¼ C. buttermilk
- ½ C. Louisiana Fish Fry
- 1 pound deveined shrimp
- Remoulade sauce:
- 1 chopped green onion
- 1 tsp. hot sauce
- 1 tsp. Dijon mustard
- ½ tsp. creole seasoning
- 1 tsp. Worcestershire sauce
- Juice of ½ a lemon
- ½ C. vegan mayo

Directions:
1. To make the sauce, combine all sauce ingredients until well incorporated. Chill while you cook shrimp.
2. Mix seasonings together and liberally season shrimp.
3. Add buttermilk to a bowl. Dip each shrimp into milk and place in a Ziploc bag. Chill half an hour to marinate.
4. Insert the Crisper Basket, and close the hood. Select AIR CRISP, set the temperature to 400°F, and set the time to 10 minutes. Select START/STOP to begin preheating.
5. Add fish fry to a bowl. Take shrimp from marinating bag and dip into fish fry, then add to the crisper basket.
6. Spray shrimp with olive oil.
7. Air Frying.
8. Cook 5 minutes, flip and then cook another 5 minutes. Assemble "Keto" Po Boy by adding sauce to lettuce leaves, along with shrimp and tomato.

Nutrition: Calories 337   Carbs 6 g   Fat 12 g   Protein 24 g   Sugar 2 g

Seared Sea Scallops With Roasted Garlic And Dill Butter

Preparation Time: 5 minutes   Cooking Tim e **:** 3 minutes
Serving: 6

Ingredients:
- 12–18 medium-sized scallops
- 1 tsp. kosher salt
- 1 lemon
- 2 Tbsp. roasted garlic and dill butter
- 2 tsp. olive oil

Directions :

1. Insert the Cooking Pot and close the hood. Select GRILL, set temperature to HIGH, and set time to 8 minutes. Select START/STOP to begin preheating.
2. Rinse scallops in cold water and dry thoroughly with a paper towel.
3. Season scallops lightly with kosher salt.
4. Slice lemon into ¼-inch thick slices and remove seeds.
5. Melt in the cooking pot butter and olive oil in pan.
6. Gently place the scallops and lemon slices into the oil and butter. Be careful not to let the scallops touch each other in the pot.
7. Select BAKE and Sear for 90 seconds on each side. A nice crust will form on both sides of the scallop, with the middle remaining relatively opaque.
8. Serve hot.

Scallops and Spring Veggies

Preparation Time: 10 minutes   **Cooking Time:** 10 minutes

Serving: 4

Ingredients :
- ½ pound asparagus, ends trimmed, cut into 2-inch pieces
- 1 cup sugar snap peas
- 1 pound sea scallops
- 1 tablespoon lemon juice
- 2 teaspoons olive oil
- ½ teaspoon dried thyme
- Pinch salt
- Freshly ground black pepper

Directions:
1. Insert the Crisper Basket, and close the hood. Select AIR CRISP, set the temperature to 355°F, and set the time to 10 minutes. Select START/STOP to begin preheating.
2. Place the asparagus and sugar snap peas in the crisper basket.
3. Air Frying.
4. Cook for 2 to 3 minutes or until the vegetables are just starting to get tender.
5. Meanwhile, check the scallops for a small muscle attached to the side, and pull it off and discard.
6. In a medium bowl, toss the scallops with the lemon juice, olive oil, thyme, salt, and pepper. Place into the crisper basket on top of the vegetables.
7. Air Frying.
8. Steam for 5 to 7 minutes, tossing the basket once during cooking time, until the scallops are just firm when tested with your finger and are opaque in the center, and the vegetables are tender. Serve immediately.

Nutrition:
Calories 162   Carbs 10 g   Fat 4 g   Protein 22 g   Fiber 3 g

Tuna With Fresh Tomato-Basil Sauce

Preparation Time: 5 minutes   **Cooking Time:** 20 minutes

Serving: 4

Ingredients :
- TOMATO-BASIL SAUCE
- 2 tablespoons olive oil
- 1 small yellow onion, diced
- ¼ teaspoon salt
- ½ pint cherry tomatoes, cut in half
- 2 tablespoons water
- ¼ cup fresh basil leaves, chopped
- TUNA
- 1 tablespoon olive oil
- 4 (6-ounce tuna steaks, about 1 inch thick

Directions :
1. In a medium saucepan, heat the olive oil over medium heat. Add the onion and salt. Cook, stirring frequently, until the onion is golden brown, 10 to 15 minutes. Add the tomatoes and water and cook for approximately 5 to 7 minutes, until the tomatoes have softened and wrinkled. (The sauce can be cooled, covered, and refrigerated overnight. Reheat before serving. Stir in the basil just before serving.
2. Insert the Grill Grate and close the hood. Select GRILL, set temperature to HIGH, and set time to 8 minutes. Select START/STOP to begin preheating.
3. Rub the olive oil over the tuna steaks. Grill for about 4 minutes. To test for doneness, prod on edge of the tuna with a fork. The fish should flake, but the center will still be a bit rosy.
4. Spoon the tuna into 4 shallow bowls and top with the warm tomato-basil sauce.

Nutrition:
Calories 289   Fat 12 g   Protein 40 g   Sugar 4 g

Tuna Stuffed Potatoes

Preparation Time: 5 minutes   **Cooking Time:** 30 minutes
Serving: 4

Ingredients:
- 4 starchy potatoes
- ½ tablespoon olive oil
- 1 (6-ounce can tuna, drained
- 2 tablespoons plain Greek yogurt
- 1 teaspoon red chili powder
- Salt and freshly ground black pepper, to taste
- 1 scallion, chopped and divided
- 1 tablespoon caper

Directions:
1. In a large bowl of water, soak the potatoes for about 30 minutes. Drain well and pat dry with paper towel.
2. Insert the Crisper Basket, and close the hood. Select AIR CRISP, set the temperature to 355°F, and set the time to 30 minutes. Select START/STOP to begin preheating and place the potatoes in the crisper basket.
3. Air Frying.
4. Cook for about 30 minutes.
5. Meanwhile in a bowl, add tuna, yogurt, red chili powder, salt, black pepper and half of scallion and with a potato masher, mash the mixture completely.
6. Remove the potatoes from the air fryer and place onto a smooth surface.
7. Carefully, cut each potato from top side lengthwise.
8. With your fingers, press the open side of potato halves slightly. Stuff the potato open portion with tuna mixture evenly.
9. Sprinkle with the capers and remaining scallion. Serve immediately.

Salmon Noodles

Preparation Time: 5 minutes   **Cooking Time:** 16 minutes
Serving: 4

Ingredients:
- 1 Salmon Fillet
- 1 Tbsp Teriyaki Marinade
- 3 ½ Ozs Soba Noodles, cooked and drained
- 10 Ozs Firm Tofu
- 7 Ozs Mixed Salad
- 1 Cup Broccoli
- Olive Oil
- Salt and Pepper to taste

Directions:
1. Season the salmon with salt and pepper to taste, then coat with the teriyaki marinate. Set aside for 15 minutes.
2. Insert the Crisper Basket, and close the hood. Select AIR CRISP, set the temperature to 350°F, and set the time to 16 minutes. Select START/STOP to begin preheating.
3. Air Frying.
4. Cook the salmon for 8 minutes.
5. Whilst the air fryer is cooking the salmon, start slicing the tofu into small cubes.
6. Next, slice the broccoli into smaller chunks. Drizzle with olive oil.
7. Once the salmon is cooked, put the broccoli and tofu into the crisper basket tray for 8 minutes.
8. Plate the salmon and broccoli tofu mixture over the soba noodles. Add the mixed salad to the side and serve

Fried Calamari

Preparation Time: 8 minutes   **Cooking Time:** 15 minutes

Serving: 6-8

Ingredients :
- ½ tsp. salt
- ½ tsp. Old Bay seasoning
- 1/3 C. plain cornmeal
- ½ C. semolina flour
- ½ C. almond flour
- 5-6 C. olive oil
- 1 ½ pounds baby squid

Directions:
1. Rinse squid in cold water and slice tentacles, keeping just ¼-inch of the hood in one piece.
2. Insert the Crisper Basket, and close the hood. Select AIR CRISP, set the temperature to 345°F, and set the time to 15 minutes. Select START/STOP to begin preheating.
3. Combine 1-2 pinches of pepper, salt, Old Bay seasoning, cornmeal, and both flours together. Dredge squid pieces into flour mixture and place into the crisper basket.
4. Air frying. Spray liberally with olive oil. Cook 15 minutes at 345 degrees till coating turns a golden brown.

Nutrition:
Calories 211   Fat 6 g   Protein 21 g   Sugar 1 g

POULTRY

Grilled Stuffed Pork Tenderloin

Preparation Time: 5 minutes   **Cooking Time:** 30 minutes
Serving: 4

Ingredients :
- 1½ Tbsp. olive oil, plus a drizzle
- ½ medium Vidalia onion, finely chopped
- 1 tsp. Worcestershire sauce
- 6oz. chopped baby bella mushrooms
- 2 cloves garlic, minced
- 2 tsp. minced rosemary
- 4 fresh sage leaves, chopped
- ½ tsp. celery salt
- ½ tsp. fresh black pepper
- ¼ cup chopped flat-leaf parsley
- 2 cups fresh spinach leaves, stems removed
- 2 tsp. Dijon mustard
- 1 pork tenderloin, 1½ to 2 lb.
- 4 slices pancetta
- 4 slices provolone cheese
- 2 tsp. rosemary salt

Directions :
1. In a medium skillet, heat olive oil over medium heat. Add onion and cook for 1 minute before adding Worcestershire sauce, mushrooms, garlic, rosemary, sage, celery salt, and black pepper. Constantly mixing with wooden spoon, cook down till mushrooms are soft (5–7 minutes.
2. Add parsley and spinach. Continue to mix with wooden spoon. Cook until spinach starts to wilt. Stir in mustard and cook for additional 1 minute. Remove from heat, set aside, and allow to cool while you prep the pork.
3. Insert the Grill Grate and close the hood. Select GRILL, set the temperature to MEDIUM, and set the time to 15 minutes. Select START/STOP to begin preheating. Place pork tenderloin on cutting board, and with your knife parallel to the cutting surface, roll cut the tenderloin so it's about ½-inch thick when unrolled.
4. Once pork has been roll cut, lay pancetta on top, followed by provolone cheese and spinach mixture. Leave about a 1-inch border around the edge of the loin.
5. Roll tenderloin back up and truss together with butcher's twine. (If you're not sure how to truss, just tie the roll up using a simple square knot every 2 inches, but trussing is super easy. Drizzle outside of roll with a very thin coat of olive oil and sprinkle with rosemary salt.
6. When the unit beeps to signify it has preheated, place the pork on the Grill Grate. Close the hood and cook for 11 minutes. After 11 minutes, flip the pork, close the hood, and cook for an additional 11 minutes. Remove from grill, slice, and serve.

Grill Pork Quesadilla

Preparation Time: 10 minutes   Cooking Time : 12 minutes
Serving: 2

Ingredients :
- Two 6-inch corn or flour tortilla shells
- 1 medium-sized pork shoulder, approximately 4 ounces, sliced
- ½ medium-sized white onion, sliced
- ½ medium-sized red pepper, sliced
- ½ medium sized green pepper, sliced
- ½ medium sized yellow pepper, sliced
- ¼ cup of shredded pepper-jack cheese
- ¼ cup of shredded mozzarella cheese

Directions:
1. Insert the Grill Grate and close the hood. Select GRILL, set the temperature to HIGH, and set the time to 20 minutes. Select START/STOP to begin preheating.
2. Grill the pork, onion, and peppers in foil in the same grill grate, allowing the moisture from the vegetables and the juice from the pork mingle together. Remove pork and vegetables. While they're cooling, sprinkle half the shredded cheese over one of the tortillas, then cover with the pieces of pork, onions, and peppers, and then layer on the rest of the shredded cheese. Top with the second tortilla. Place directly on hot surface of the grill grate.
3. Set the temperature to MED, and set the timer for 6 minutes. After 6 minutes, when the shuts off, flip the tortillas onto the other side with a spatula; the cheese should be melted enough that it won't fall apart, but be careful anyway not to spill any toppings.
4. Reset to 350 degrees for another 6 minutes.
5. After 6 minutes, when shuts off, the tortillas should be browned and crisp, and the pork, onion, peppers and cheese will be crispy and hot and delicious. Remove with tongs and let sit on a serving plate to cool for a few minutes before slicing.

Roasted Pork Tenderloin

Preparation Time: 5 minutes   **Cooking Time:** 1 hour

Serving: 4

Ingredients :
- 1 (3-pound pork tenderloin
- 2 tablespoons extra-virgin olive oil
- 2 garlic cloves, minced
- 1 teaspoon dried basil
- 1 teaspoon dried oregano
- 1 teaspoon dried thyme
- Salt
- Pepper

Directions:
1. Drizzle the pork tenderloin with the olive oil.
2. Rub the garlic, basil, oregano, thyme, and salt and pepper to taste all over the tenderloin.
3. Insert the Crisper Basket, and close the hood. Select AIR CRISP, set the temperature to 330°F, and set the time to 45 minutes. Select START/STOP to begin preheating.
4. Air frying.
5. Place the tenderloin in the Crisper basket. Cook for 45 minutes.
6. Use a meat thermometer to test for doneness
7. Open the air fryer and flip the pork tenderloin. Cook for an additional 15 minutes.
8. Remove the cooked pork from the air fryer and allow it to rest for 10 minutes before cutting.

Nutrition: Calories 283   Fat 10 g   Protein 48 g

Italian Parmesan Breaded Pork Chops

Preparation Time: 5 minutes   **Cooking Time:** 12 minutes

Serving: 5

Ingredients :
- 5 (3½- to 5-ounce pork chops (bone-in or boneless
- 1 teaspoon Italian seasoning
- Seasoning salt
- Pepper
- ¼ cup all-purpose flour
- 2 tablespoons Italian bread crumbs
- 3 tablespoons finely grated Parmesan cheese
- Cooking oil

Directions:

1. Season the pork chops with the Italian seasoning and seasoning salt and pepper to taste.
2. Sprinkle the flour on both sides of the pork chops, then coat both sides with the bread crumbs and Parmesan cheese.
3. Insert the Crisper Basket, and close the hood. Select AIR CRISP, set the temperature to 330°F, and set the time to 15 minutes. Select START/STOP to begin preheating.
4. Air frying.
5. Place the pork chops in the crisper basket. Stacking them is okay. Spray the pork chops with cooking oil. Cook for 6 minutes.
6. Open the air fryer and flip the pork chops. Cook for an additional 6 minutes.
7. Cool before serving. Instead of seasoning salt, you can use either chicken or pork rub for additional flavor. You can find these rubs in the spice aisle of the grocery store.

Nutrition: Calories 334   Fat 7 g   Protein 34 g   Sugar

Korean Spicy Pork

Preparation Time: 5 minutes   **Cooking Time:** 3 minutes

Serving: 4

Ingredients:
- 2 lbs. pork, cut into ⅛-inch slices
- ½ cup soy sauce
- 5 cloves garlic, minced
- 3 Tbsp. minced green onion
- 1 yellow onion, sliced
- 2 Tbsp. sesame seeds
- 3 tsp. black pepper
- ½ cup brown sugar
- 3 Tbsp. gochujang (Korean red chili paste
- red pepper flakes to taste

Directions:
1. Mix all the ingredients together in a covered glass bowl or resealable bag and refrigerate for several hours to overnight.
2. Insert the Grill Grate and close the hood. Select GRILL, set the temperature to MEDIUM, and set the time to 8 minutes. Select START/STOP to begin preheating.
3. Grill the pork for 2–3 minutes per side until it is cooked through.
4. Serve immediately on rice or lettuce leaves with soy and/or kimchi.

Chinese Salt and Pepper Pork Chop Stir-fry

Preparation Time: 10 minutes   **Cooking Time:** 15 minutes
Serving: 4

Ingredients :
- Pork Chops:
- Olive oil
- ¾ C. almond flour
- ¼ tsp. pepper
- ½ tsp. salt
- 1 egg white
- Pork Chops
- Stir-fry:
- ¼ tsp. pepper
- 1 tsp. sea salt
- 2 tbsp. olive oil
- 2 sliced scallions
- 2 sliced jalapeno peppers

Directions:

1. Insert the Crisper Basket, and close the hood. Select AIR CRISP, set the temperature to 360°F, and set the time to 12 minutes. Select START/STOP to begin preheating.
2. Coat the crisper basket with olive oil.
3. Whisk pepper, salt, and egg white together till foamy.
4. Cut pork chops into pieces, leaving just a bit on bones. Pat dry.
5. Add pieces of pork to egg white mixture, coating well. Let sit for marinade 20 minutes.
6. Put marinated chops into a large bowl and add almond flour. Dredge and shake off excess and place into air fryer.
7. Air frying. Cook 12 minutes at 360 degrees.
8. Turn up the heat to 400 degrees and cook another 6 minutes till pork chops are nice and crisp.
9. To make stir-fry, remove jalapeno seeds and chop up. Chop scallions and mix with jalapeno pieces.
10. Heat a skillet with olive oil. Stir-fry pepper, salt, scallions, and jalapenos 60 seconds. Then add fried pork pieces to skills and toss with scallion mixture. Stir-fry 1-2 minutes till well coated and hot.

Nutrition:
Calories 294   Fat 17 g   Protein 36 g   Sugar 4 g

Garlic Putter Pork Chops

Preparation Time: 10 minutes   **Cooking Time:** 15 minutes

Serving: 4

Ingredients :
- 2 tsp. parsley
- 2 tsp. grated garlic cloves
- 1 tbsp. coconut oil
- 1 tbsp. coconut butter
- 4 pork chops

Directions:
1. Mix butter, coconut oil, and all seasoning together. Then rub seasoning mixture over all sides of pork chops. Place in foil, seal, and chill for 1 hour.
2. Insert the Crisper Basket, and close the hood. Select AIR CRISP, set the temperature to 350°F, and set the time to 15 minutes. Select START/STOP to begin preheating.
3. Remove pork chops from foil and place into the crisper basket.
4. Air frying. Set temperature to 350°F, and set time to 7 minutes. Cook 7 minutes on one side and 8 minutes on the other.
5. Drizzle with olive oil and serve alongside a green salad.

Nutrition: Calories 526   Fat 23 g   Protein 41 g   Sugar 4 g

Fried Pork with Sweet and Sour Glaze

Preparation Time: 5 minutes   **Cooking Time:** 30 minutes

Serving: 4

Ingredients :
- ¼ cup rice wine vinegar
- ¼ teaspoon Chinese five spice powder
- 1 cup potato starch
- 1 green onion, chopped
- 2 large eggs, beaten
- 2 pounds pork chops cut into chunks
- 2 tablespoons cornstarch + 3 tablespoons water
- 5 tablespoons brown sugar
- Salt and pepper to taste

Directions:

1. Insert the Crisper Basket, and close the hood. Select AIR CRISP, set the temperature to 390°F, and set the time to 30 minutes. Select START/STOP to begin preheating.
2. Season pork chops with salt and pepper to taste.
3. Dip the pork chops in egg. Set aside.
4. In a bowl, combine the potato starch and Chinese five spice powder.
5. Dredge the pork chops in the flour mixture.
6. Air frying. Place in the Crisper Basket and cook for 30 minutes.
7. Meanwhile, place the vinegar and brown sugar in a saucepan. Season with salt and pepper to taste. Stir in the cornstarch slurry and allow to simmer until thick.
8. Serve the pork chops with the sauce and garnish with green onions.

Nutrition: Calories 420   Fat 12 g   Protein 70 g

Molasses BBQ Pork Chops

Preparation Time: 5 minutes   **Cooking Time:** 4 minutes
Serving: 4
Ingredients

MOLASSES BARBECUE SAUCE
- 2 tablespoons molasses
- 2 tablespoons ketchup
- 1 tablespoon cider vinegar
- 1 teaspoon light brown sugar
- ¼ teaspoon salt
- Pinch of ground cloves
- Pinch of sweet paprika

PORK : 4 (6-ounce boneless center-cut pork chops, pounded to ½-inch thickness

Directions
1. Whisk together the molasses, ketchup, vinegar, brown sugar, salt, cloves, and paprika in a small bowl. (The sauce can be covered with plastic wrap and refrigerated for up to 3 days.
2. Insert the Grill Grate and close the hood. Select GRILL, set the temperature to MEDIUM, and set the time to 8 minutes. Select START/STOP to begin preheating.
3. Pour the sauce into a shallow baking dish. Add the chops and turn to coat. Grill the chops for about 4 minutes, until they have taken on grill marks and are firm to the touch. Serve immediately.

Nutrition: Calories 283   Fat 4 g   Protein 37 g

Pork Cutlet Rolls

Preparation Time: 10 minutes   **Cooking Time:** 15 minutes

Serving: 4

Ingredients :
- 4 Pork Cutlets
- 4 Sundried Tomatoes in oil
- 2 Tbsps Parsley, finely chopped
- 1 Green Onion, finely chopped
- Black Pepper to taste
- 2 Tsps Paprika
- 1/2 Tbsp Olive Oil
- * String for Rolled Meat

Directions:
1. Insert the Crisper Basket, and close the hood. Select AIR CRISP, set the temperature to 390°F, and set the time to 15 minutes. Select START/STOP to begin preheating.
2. Finely chop the tomatoes and mix with the parsley and green onion. Add salt and pepper to taste
3. Spread out the cutlets and coat them with the tomato mixture. Roll up the cutlets and secure intact with the string
4. Rub the rolls with salt, pepper, and paprika powder and thinly coat them with olive oil
5. Air frying. Put the cutlet rolls in the crisper Basket tray and cook for 15 minutes. Roast until nicely brown and done.
6. Serve with tomato sauce.

Sweet And Salty Lemongrass Pork Chops

Preparation Time: 5 minutes   **Cooking Time:** 5 minutes

Serving: 4

Ingredients :
- ¼ cup sugar
- ¼ cup oyster sauce
- ¼ cup soy sauce
- 1 teaspoon freshly ground black pepper
- 2 stalks lemongrass, or 2 strips of lemon zest
- 4 cloves garlic, peeled and gently crushed with the side of a cleaver
- 4 boneless pork loin chops (each ¼ to ½ inch thick, and about 1½ pounds total

Directions :
1. Place the sugar, oyster sauce, soy sauce, and pepper in a large shallow mixing bowl and whisk until the sugar dissolves.
2. Trim the lemongrass, removing the root ends and flexible green stalks. You should be left with a cream-colored core that is 3 to 4 inches long. Cut this into 1-inch pieces and gently crush them with the side of a cleaver to release the aroma. Stir the lemongrass and garlic into the marinade.
3. Add the pork chops to the marinade, turning to coat both sides. Cover the bowl with plastic wrap and let the pork chops marinate in the refrigerator for at least 2 hours or as long as overnight, turning them several times; the longer the chops marinate, the richer the flavor will be. You can also marinate the chops in a resealable plastic bag.
4. Insert the Grill Grate and close the hood. Select GRILL, set the temperature to MEDIUM, and set the time to 8 minutes. Select START/STOP to begin preheating.
5. Place the pork chops on the hot grill, then close the hood. The chops will be done after cooking 2 to 4 minutes.
6. To test for doneness, use the poke method; the meat should be firm but gently yielding.
7. Transfer the pork chops to a platter or plates and serve at once.

Dijon Garlic Pork Tenderloin

Preparation Time: 5 minutes   **Cooking Time:** 15 minutes

Serving: 4

Ingredients :
- 1 C. breadcrumbs
- Pinch of cayenne pepper
- 3 crushed garlic cloves
- 2 tbsp. ground ginger
- 2 tbsp. Dijon mustard
- 2 tbsp. raw honey
- 4 tbsp. water
- 2 tsp. salt
- 1pound pork tenderloin, sliced into 1-inch rounds

Directions:
1. Insert the Crisper Basket, and close the hood. Select AIR CRISP, set the temperature to 400°F, and set the time to 10 minutes. Select START/STOP to begin preheating.
2. With pepper and salt, season all sides of tenderloin.
3. Combine cayenne pepper, garlic, ginger, mustard, honey, and water until smooth.
4. Dip pork rounds into honey mixture and then into breadcrumbs, ensuring they all get coated well.
5. Place coated pork rounds into the Crisper Basket.
6. Air frying. Cook 10 minutes at 400 degrees. Flip and then cook an additional 5 minutes until golden in color.

Nutrition:

Calories 423   Fat 18 g   Protein 31 g   Sugar 3 g

Air Fryer Sweet and Sour Pork

Preparation Time: 10 minutes   **Cooking Time:** 12 minutes

Serving: 5

Ingredients :
- 3 tbsp. olive oil
- 1/16 tsp. Chinese Five Spice
- ¼ tsp. pepper
- ½ tsp. sea salt
- 1 tsp. pure sesame oil
- 2 eggs
- 1 C. almond flour
- 2 pounds pork, sliced into chunks
- Sweet and Sour Sauce:
- ¼ tsp. sea salt
- ½ tsp. garlic powder
- 1 tbsp. low-sodium soy sauce
- ½ C. rice vinegar
- 5 tbsp. tomato paste
- 1/8 tsp. water
- ½ C. sweetener of choice

Directions:
1. Insert the Crisper Basket, and close the hood. Select AIR CRISP, set the temperature to 340°F, and set the time to 12 minutes. Select START/STOP to begin preheating.
2. To make the dipping sauce, whisk all sauce ingredients together over medium heat, stirring 5 minutes. Simmer uncovered 5 minutes till thickened.
3. Meanwhile, combine almond flour, five spice, pepper, and salt.
4. In another bowl, mix eggs with sesame oil.
5. Dredge pork in flour mixture and then in egg mixture. Shake any excess off before adding to air fryer basket.
6. Air frying. Cook 12 minutes at 340 degrees.
7. Serve with sweet and sour dipping sauce.

Nutrition: Calories 371   Fat 17 g   Protein 27 g   Sugar 1 g

Fried Pork Scotch Egg

Preparation Time: 10 minutes   Cooking Time: 25 minutes
Serving: 2

Ingredients:
- 3 soft-boiled eggs, peeled
- 8 ounces of raw minced pork, or sausage outside the casings
- 2 teaspoons of ground rosemary
- 2 teaspoons of garlic powder
- Pinch of salt and pepper
- 2 raw eggs
- 1 cup of breadcrumbs (Panko, but other brands are fine, or home-made bread crumbs work too)

Directions:
1. Cover the Crisper basket with a lining of tin foil, leaving the edges uncovered to allow air to circulate through the basket. Insert the Crisper Basket, and close the hood. Select AIR CRISP, set the temperature to 350°F, and set the time to 25 minutes. Select START/STOP to begin preheating.
2. In a mixing bowl, combine the raw pork with the rosemary, garlic powder, salt and pepper. This will probably be easiest to do with your masher or bare hands (though make sure to wash thoroughly after handling raw meat; combine until all the spices are evenly spread throughout the meat.
3. Divide the meat mixture into three equal portions in the mixing bowl, and form each into balls with your hands.
4. Lay a large sheet of plastic wrap on the countertop, and flatten one of the balls of meat on top of it, to form a wide, flat meat-circle.
5. Place one of the peeled soft-boiled eggs in the center of the meat-circle and then, using the ends of the plastic wrap, pull the meat-circle so that it is fully covering and surrounding the soft-boiled egg.
6. Tighten and shape the plastic wrap covering the meat so that if forms a ball, and make sure not to squeeze too hard lest you squish the soft-boiled egg at the center of the ball! Set aside.
7. Repeat with the other two soft-boiled eggs and portions of meat-mixture.
8. In a separate mixing bowl, beat the two raw eggs until fluffy and until the yolks and whites are fully combined.One by one, remove the plastic wrap and dunk the pork-covered balls into the raw egg, and then roll them in the bread crumbs, covering fully and generously.
9. Place each of the bread-crumb covered meat-wrapped balls onto the foil-lined surface of the air fryer. Three of them should fit nicely, without touching.Air Frying.
10. Cook 25 minutes at 350 degrees. About halfway through the cooking time, shake the handle of the air-fryer vigorously, so that the scotch eggs inside roll around and ensure full coverage.
11. After 25 minutes, the air fryer will shut off and the scotch eggs should be perfect – the meat fully cooked, the egg-yolks still runny on the inside, and the outsides crispy and golden-brown.

Roasted Char Siew (Pork Butt)

Preparation Time: 10 minutes   **Cooking Time:** 25 minutes

Serving: 6

Ingredients :
- 1 strip of pork shoulder butt with a good amount of fat marbling
- Marinade:
- 1 tsp. sesame oil
- 4 tbsp. raw honey
- 1 tsp. low-sodium dark soy sauce
- 1 tsp. light soy sauce
- 1 tbsp. rose wine
- 2 tbsp. Hoisin sauce

Directions:
1. Combine all marinade ingredients together and add to Ziploc bag. Place pork in bag, making sure all sections of pork strip are engulfed in the marinade. Chill 3-24 hours.
2. Insert the Crisper Basket, and close the hood. Select AIR CRISP, set the temperature to 350°F, and set the time to 20 minutes. Select START/STOP to begin preheating.
3. Place foil on small pan and brush with olive oil. Place marinated pork strip onto prepared pan.
4. Air frying. Set temperature to 350°F, and set time to 20 minutes. Roast 20 minutes.
5. Glaze with marinade every 5-10 minutes.
6. Remove strip and leave to cool a few minutes before slicing.

Nutrition: Calories 289   Fat 13 g   Protein 33 g   Sugar 1 g

Wonton Taco Cups

Preparation Time: 5 minutes   Cooking Time: 10 minutes

Serving: 8

Ingredients :
- 1/2 pound ground pork, browned and drained
- 1/2 pound ground beef, browned and drained
- 1 envelope taco seasoning
- 1 (10-ounce can tomatoes with chilies, diced and drained
- 1 bell pepper, seeded and chopped
- 32 wonton wrappers
- 1 cup Cheddar cheese, shredded

Directions:
1. Insert the Crisper Basket, and close the hood. Select AIR CRISP, set the temperature to 370°F, and set the time to 10 minutes. Select START/STOP to begin preheating.
2. Combine the pork, beef, taco seasoning, diced tomatoes, and bell pepper; mix well.
3. Line all the muffin cups with wonton wrappers. Spritz with a nonstick cooking oil. Divide the beef filling among wrappers; top with the shredded cheese.
4. Air frying.
5. Bake at 370 degrees F for about 10 minutes or until heated through.

BEEF PORK AND LAMB

Cold Soba With Beef And Cucumber

Preparation Time: 5 minutes   Cooking Tim e : 3 minutes   **Serving:** 4

Ingredients :
- SOBA
- 8 ounces soba noodles
- 1 tablespoon sesame oil
- STEAK AND DRESSING
- ¾ cup rice vinegar
- 1 tablespoon Asian sesame oil
- 3 garlic cloves, minced
- 1 jalapeño pepper, seeded and minced
- ½ teaspoon salt
- 1 pound flank steak, about 1 inch thick
- 3 tablespoons fresh lime juice (from 2 limes
- SALAD
- 1 large seedless cucumber, halved lengthwise and thinly sliced
- 1 ripe mango, halved and thinly sliced
- 1 cup chopped fresh basil leaves
- 1 cup chopped fresh mint leaves
- ½ cup unsalted roasted cashews, chopped
- 1 carrot, halved lengthwise and thinly sliced
- 1 teaspoon sesame seeds
- 1 scallion, chopped

Directions :
1. Bring a medium saucepan of water to a boil. Add the soba and cook for about 3 to 5 minutes until it is al dente-soft with just a little firmness left. Drain, rinse with cold water, and transfer to a medium serving bowl. Toss with the sesame oil, cover with plastic wrap, and refrigerate for at least 2 hours or overnight.
2. Combine the rice vinegar, sesame oil, garlic, jalapeño, and salt in a shallow baking dish. Add the steak, turning to coat. Cover with plastic wrap and refrigerate for at least 2 hours or overnight.
3. Insert the Grill Grate and close the hood. Select GRILL, set temperature to HIGH, and set time to 5 minutes. Select START/STOP to begin preheating. Remove the steak from the marinade, and reserve the marinade in a small saucepan. Grill the steak for about 5 minutes for medium-rare. It should have grill marks and feel fairly firm to the touch. Let the steak rest on a cutting board for about 5 minutes.
4. Bring the marinade to a boil, cook for 1 minute, then remove from the heat. Pour into a small bowl, stir in the lime juice, and refrigerate the dressing to cool while you prepare the salad.
5. Seedless cucumbers are available in supermarkets, but you can easily remove the seeds from the standard variety: after peeling, cut the cucumber in half lengthwise. Use a teaspoon to scoop out the middle core of seeds.
6. Add the dressing to the soba noodles and toss thoroughly. Add the cucumber, mango, basil, and mint and toss gently to combine.
7. Thinly slice the steak across the grain and arrange over the noodles. Sprinkle the cashews and chopped scallion over the top. Serve immediately.

Beef Ribeye Steak

Preparation Time: 5 minutes   **Cooking Tim e :** 20 minutes

Serving: 4

Ingredients :
- 4 (8-ounce ribeye steaks
- 1 tablespoon McCormick Grill Mates Montreal Steak Seasoning
- Salt
- Pepper

Directions:
1. Insert the Grill Grate and close the hood. Select GRILL, set temperature to HIGH, and set time to 10 minutes. Select START/STOP to begin preheating. Season the steaks with the steak seasoning and salt and pepper to taste. Place 2 steaks in the grill grate.
2. Cook for 4 minutes. Open the hood and flip the steaks.
3. Cook for an additional 4 to 5 minutes. Check for doneness to determine how much additional cook time is need. Remove the cooked steaks from the grill, then repeat steps for the remaining 2 steaks. Cool before serving.

Nutrition:
Calories: 293;   Fat: 22G;   Protein:23G;   Fiber:0G   Calories 293   Fat 22 g   Protein 32 g

Filets Mignons With Gaucho Seasonings

Preparation Time: 5 minutes   **Cooking Time:** 10 minutes

Serving: 4

Ingredients :
- 1 clove garlic, minced
- Coarse salt (kosher or sea and freshly ground black pepper
- 1 tablespoon dried oregano
- 1 teaspoon dried sage
- 2 tablespoons distilled white vinegar or wine vinegar, or more to taste
- 2 tablespoons extra-virgin olive oil
- 2 tablespoons boiling water
- 1½ pounds filet mignon

Directions :
1. Place the garlic, 1 teaspoon of salt, and ½ teaspoon of pepper in a small, heatproof bowl and mash to a paste with the back of a spoon. Add the oregano and sage and continue mashing until combined. Add the vinegar and whisk to

mix. Whisk in the olive oil, followed by the boiling water. Taste for seasoning, adding more salt, pepper, and/or vinegar as necessary; the sauce should be highly seasoned. Season the fillets with salt and pepper.
2. Preheat the grill to high. When the unit beeps to signify it has preheated, add the filets to the Grill Grate. Gently press the filets down to maximize grill marks, then close the hood. After 4 minutes, open the hood and flip the filets. Close the hood and continue cooking for an additional 4 minutes, or until the filets' internal temperature reads 125°F on a food thermometer. Remove the filets from the grill; they will continue to cook (called carry-over cooking to a food-safe temperature even after you've removed them from the grill.
3. Let the filets rest for a total of 10 minutes; this allows the natural juices to redistribute into the steak.

Chili-Espresso Marinated Steak

Preparation Time: 5 minutes   Cooking Tim e : 50 minutes
Serving: 3
Ingredients :
- ½ teaspoon garlic powder
- 1 ½ pounds beef flank steak
- 1 teaspoon instant espresso powder
- 2 tablespoons olive oil
- 2 teaspoons chili powder
- Salt and pepper to taste

Directions:
1. Insert the Grill Grate and close the hood. Select GRILL, set temperature to HIGH, and set time to 40 minutes. Select START/STOP to begin preheating.
2. Make the dry rub by mixing the chili powder, salt, pepper, espresso powder, and garlic powder.
3. Rub all over the steak and brush with oil.
4. Place on the grill grate and cook for 40 minutes.
5. Halfway through the cooking time, flip the beef to cook evenly.

Nutrition : Calories 249   Fat 17 g   Protein 20 g   Sugar 2 g

Marinated London Broil

Preparation Time: 5 minutes **Cooking Time:** 4 minutes

Serving: 4

Ingredients :
- 2-lb. London broil
- MARINADE
- ½ cup soy sauce
- 2 Tbsp. balsamic vinegar
- 2 Tbsp. Dijon mustard
- 4 cloves garlic, minced
- 2 Tbsp. olive oil
- 3 sprigs fresh rosemary
- 1 tsp. coarsely ground black pepper

Directions:
1. Combine all marinade ingredients in mixing bowl and whisk together.
2. Using a sharp knife, cut a diamond, or crosshatch, pattern into each side of the meat, only cutting about ¼ inch deep. This will allow the marinade to penetrate the meat deeper in a shorter amount of time.
3. Place meat in sealable plastic bag and cover with marinade. Place in refrigerator for 2 hours.
4. After 2 hours, remove from refrigerator and allow to come up to room temperature for 1 hour.
5. Insert the Grill Grate and close the hood. Select GRILL, set temperature to HIGH, and set time to 8 minutes. Select START/STOP to begin preheating.
6. Remove meat from marinade and pat dry with paper towel. Grill over high heat. Let cook for 2 minutes, rotate 90 degrees, and allow to cook for another 2 minutes.
7. Flip meat and repeat.
8. Remove from grill when internal temperature reaches 125°F. Tent with foil and let rest for 5 minutes before slicing.
9. Serve with chipotle aioli

Cumin-Paprika Rubbed Beef Brisket

Preparation Time: 5 minutes   **Cooking Time:** 2 hours   **Serving:** 12

Ingredients :
- ¼ teaspoon cayenne pepper
- 1 ½ tablespoons paprika
- 1 teaspoon garlic powder
- 1 teaspoon ground cumin
- 1 teaspoon onion powder
- 2 teaspoons dry mustard
- 2 teaspoons ground black pepper
- 2 teaspoons salt
- 5 pounds brisket roast
- 5 tablespoons olive oil

Directions:
1. Place all ingredients in a Ziploc bag and allow to marinate in the fridge for at least 2 hours.
2. Remove the Grill Grate from the unit. Select BAKE, set the temperature to 350°F, and set the time to 30 minutes. Select START/STOP to begin preheating and cook for 2 hours at 350°F.

Nutrition:
Calories 268   Fat 13 g   Protein 36 g   Fiber 3 g

Beef Bulgogi

Preparation Time: 5 minutes   **Cooking Time:** 4 minutes   **Serving:** 4

Ingredients :
- 2 lbs. flank steak
- ½ cup soy sauce
- ½ cup brown sugar
- 2 Tbsp. chopped green onion
- 4 cloves garlic, minced
- 2 Tbsp. sesame seeds
- 2 Tbsp. sesame oil
- 2 tsp. black pepper

Directions :
1. Mix all of the ingredients together in a bowl or bag and refrigerate for several hours to overnight.
2. Insert the Grill Grate and close the hood. Select GRILL, set temperature to HIGH, and set time to 8 minutes. Select START/STOP to begin preheating.
3. Add the filets to the Grill Grate. Gently press the filets down to maximize grill marks, then close the hood. After 4 minutes, open the hood and flip the filets.
4. Let rest for several minutes before slicing and serving.

Smoked Meat Loaf

Preparation Time: 5 minutes   **Cooking Time:** 25 minutes

Serving: 4

Ingredients :
- 2 Tbsp. olive oil
- 1 medium sweet onion, chopped
- 1/2 cup chopped celery
- 1/4 cup diced red bell pepper
- 1/4 cup diced yellow bell pepper
- 5 slices white bread
- ½ cup buttermilk
- 1 package dried onion soup mix
- 1.5 lb. ground beef (80/20
- 1 lb. ground Italian sausage
- 2 Tbsp. Worcestershire sauce
- 1½ cups BBQ sauce, divided in half
- 2 large eggs

Directions :
1. Heat olive oil in a pan over medium heat and sauté the chopped onion, celery, and peppers for about 5 minutes or until onions become translucent. Remove and set aside.
2. Tear the bread into small chunks and soak in buttermilk. These soaked pieces will keep your meat loaf moist as it cooks because, let's face it, there's not much worse than a dry meat loaf.
3. In large mixing bowl, combine soup mix with ground beef and sausage. Mix by hand until it's thoroughly incorporated.
4. Add to the meat mixture the sautéed ingredients, soaked bread chunks, Worcestershire sauce, ¾ cup of the BBQ sauce, and eggs
5. On a sheet of tinfoil, form the mixture into a loaf roughly 6 in. long, 4 in. wide, and 2 in. thick. Place in the freezer for about 15 minutes, just to firm it up.
6. Insert the Grill Grate and close the hood. Select GRILL, set temperature to HIGH, and set time to 20 minutes. Select START/STOP to begin preheating.
7. Place the Roasting Rack in the Cooking Pot and set up for indirect heat at 250°F, adding a few chunks of mild wood for smoke. Use apple or pecan for this.
8. Transfer chilled meat loaf from tinfoil to cooling rack, and place rack into preheated grill.
9. When the internal temperature of your loaf gets to 150°F, glaze it with remaining BBQ sauce and crank grill temperature up to 350°F. Continue cooking for about 10 minutes. This temperature allows the sauce to set up and get that beautiful color.
10. Remove from grill when the meat loaf temperature reaches 160°F internal temperature

Beef with Pesto

Preparation Time: 10 minutes   **Cooking Time:** 14 minutes

Serving: 4

Ingredients :
- 4 cups penne pasta, uncooked
- 10 oz. fresh baby spinach, chopped
- 4 beef (6 oz. tenderloin steaks
- 1/2 teaspoon salt
- 1/2 teaspoon pepper
- 4 cups grape tomatoes, halved
- 1/2 cup chopped walnuts
- 2/3 cup pesto
- 1/2 cup crumbled feta cheese

Direction:
1. At first, prepared the pasta as per the given instructions on the pack.
2. Drain and rinse, then keep this pasta aside.
3. Now season the tenderloin steaks with salt and pepper.
4. Prepare and preheat the Ninja Foodi Grill on a High-temperature setting.
5. Once it is preheated, open the lid and place the steaks on the grill.
6. Cover the Ninja Foodi Grill's lid and let it grill on the "Grilling Mode" for 7 minutes.
7. Flip the steaks and continue grilling for another 7 minutes
8. Toss the pasta with spinach, tomatoes, walnuts, and pesto in a bowl.
9. Slice the grilled steak and top the salad with the steak.
10. Garnish with cheese.
11. Enjoy.

Nutrition:
Calories 361 Total Fat 16 g Saturated Fat 5 g Cholesterol 114 mg Sodium 515 mg Total Carbs 19.3 g Fiber 0.1 g Sugar 18.2 g Protein 33.3 g

Sweet Chipotle Ribs

Preparation Time: 10 minutes   **Cooking Time:** 2 hours 5 minutes

Serving: 6

Ingredients :
- 3 lbs. baby back ribs
- Sauce/Glaze:
- 1 bottle (11.2 oz. beer
- 1 tablespoon Dijon mustard
- 1 cup barbecue sauce
- 1/3 cup honey
- 2 teaspoon ground chipotle pepper
- 1 ½ cups ketchup
- ½ small onion, chopped
- 1/4 teaspoon pepper
- 1/8 cup Worcestershire sauce
- 1 tablespoon chipotle in adobo sauce, chopped
- ½ teaspoon salt
- ½ teaspoon garlic powder

Direction:
1. First, wrap the ribs in a large foil and keep it aside.
2. Prepare and preheat the Ninja Foodi Grill on Roasting mode with medium temperature setting.
3. Once it is preheated, open the lid and place the wrapped ribs on the grill.
4. Cover the Ninja Foodi Grill's lid and let it roast for 1 ½ hour.
5. Take the rest of the ingredients in a saucepan and cook for 45 minutes on a simmer.
6. Brush the grilled ribs with the prepared sauce generously.
7. Place the ribs back into the grill and continue grilling for 10 minutes per side.
8. Serve.

Nutrition: Calories 405 Total Fat 23 g Saturated Fat 6 g Cholesterol 4 mg Sodium 227 mg Total Carbs 26 g Fiber 1 g Sugar 1 g Protein 45 g

Steak with Salsa Verde

Preparation Time: 10 minutes   **Cooking Time:** 18 minutes

Serving: 4

Ingredients :
- 2 cups salsa Verde
- 2 beef flank steak, diced
- 1/2 teaspoon salt
- 1/2 teaspoon pepper
- 1 cup fresh cilantro leaves
- 2 ripe avocados, diced
- 2 medium tomatoes, seeded and diced

Direction:
1. First, rub the steak with salt and pepper to season well.
2. Prepare and preheat the Ninja Foodi Grill on a High-temperature setting.
3. Once it is preheated, open the lid and place the bread slices in the grill.
4. Cover the Ninja Foodi Grill's lid and let it grill on the "Grilling Mode" for 9 minutes.
5. Flip and grill for another 9 minutes until al dente.
6. During this time, blend salsa with cilantro in a blender jug.
7. Slice the steak and serve with salsa, tomato, and avocado.

Nutrition: Calories 545 Total Fat 36.4 g Saturated Fat 10.1 g Cholesterol 200 mg Sodium 272 mg Total Carbs 40.7 g Fiber 0.2 g Sugar 0.1 g Protein 42.5 g

Pork with Salsa

Preparation Time: 10 minutes   **Cooking Time:** 12 minutes

Serving: 6

Ingredients :
- 2 lbs. pork tenderloin, ¾ inch slices
- 1/4 cup lime juice
- 2 tablespoons olive oil
- 2 garlic cloves, minced
- 1-1/2 teaspoons ground cumin
- 1-1/2 teaspoons dried oregano
- 1/2 teaspoon pepper
- Salsa:
- 1 jalapeno pepper, seeded and chopped
- 1 teaspoon sugar
- 1/3 cup chopped red onion
- 2 tablespoons chopped fresh mint
- 2 tablespoons lime juice
- 4 cups pears, chopped peeled
- 1 tablespoon lime zest, grated
- 1/2 teaspoon pepper

Direction:
1. Season the pork with lime juice, cumin, oregano, oil, garlic, and pepper in a suitable bowl.
2. Cover to refrigerate for overnight margination.
3. Prepare and preheat the Ninja Foodi Grill on a High-temperature setting.
4. Once it is preheated, open the lid and place the pork in the grill.
5. Cover the Ninja Foodi Grill's lid and let it grill on the "Grilling Mode" for 6 minutes.
6. Flip the pork and continue grilling for another 6 minutes until al dente.
7. Mix the pear salsa ingredients into a separate bowl.
8. Serve the sliced pork with pear salsa.

Nutrition: Calories 695 Total Fat 17.5 g Saturated Fat 4.8 g Cholesterol 283 mg Sodium 355 mg Total Carbs 26.4 g Fiber 1.8 g Sugar 0.8 g Protein 117.4 g

Sweet Ham Kabobs

Preparation Time: 10 minutes   **Cooking Time:** 7 minutes

Serving: 2

Ingredients :
- 1/2 can (20 oz. pineapple chunks
- 1/4 cup orange marmalade
- ½ green pepper, cubed
- 1/2 tablespoon mustard
- 1/8 teaspoon ground cloves
- ½ lb. ham, diced
- ¼ lb. Swiss cheese, diced

Direction:
1. Take 2 tablespoons of pineapple from pineapples in a bowl.
2. Add mustard, marmalade, and cloves mix well and keep it aside.
3. Thread the pineapple, green pepper, cheese, and ham over the skewers alternatively.
4. Prepare and preheat the Ninja Foodi Grill on the medium's temperature setting.
5. Once it is preheated, open the lid and place the ham skewers in the grill.
6. Cover the Ninja Foodi Grill's lid and let it grill on the "Grilling Mode" for 7 minutes.
7. Continue rotating the skewers every 2 minutes.
8. Pour the sauce on top and serve.

Nutrition: Calories 301 Total Fat 8.9 g Saturated Fat 4.5 g Cholesterol 57 mg Sodium 340 mg Total Carbs 24.7 g Fiber 1.2 g Sugar 1.3 g Protein 15.3 g

Steak & Bread Salad

Preparation Time: 10 minutes   **Cooking Time:** 14 minutes

Serving: 4

Ingredients :
- 1 tablespoon mustard
- 2 teaspoons packed brown sugar
- 1/2 teaspoon salt
- 1/2 teaspoon pepper
- 1 cup ranch salad dressing
- 1 beef top sirloin steak, diced
- 2 teaspoons chili powder
- 3 large tomatoes, diced
- 2 cups bread, cubed
- 2 tablespoons olive oil
- 2 tablespoons horseradish, finely grated
- 1 cucumber, chopped
- 1 red onion, thinly sliced

Direction:
1. First mix the chili powder with salt, pepper, and brown sugar in a bowl
2. Sauté the bread cubes with oil in a skillet for 10 minutes until golden.
3. Take a small bowl and mix horseradish with mustard and salad dressing.
4. Prepare and preheat the Ninja Foodi Grill on High-temperature setting.
5. Once it is preheated, open the lid and place the Steaks in the grill.
6. Cover the Ninja Foodi Grill's lid and let it grill on the "Grilling Mode" for 4 minutes.
7. Flip the steak and continue grilling for another 4 minutes.
8. Toss the sautéed bread cubes with rest o the ingredients and dressing mix in a salad bowl.
9. Slice the grilled steak and serve on top of the salad.
10. Enjoy.

Nutrition:
Calories 548 Total Fat 22.9 g Saturated Fat 9 g Cholesterol 105 mg Sodium 350 mg Total Carbs 17.5 g Sugar 10.9 g Fiber 6.3 g Protein 40.1 g

Raspberry Pork Chops

Preparation Time: 10 minutes   **Cooking Time:** 20 minutes

Serving: 2

Ingredients :
- ½ chipotle in adobo sauce, chopped
- ¼ cup raspberry preserves, seedless
- 1/4 teaspoon salt
- 2 bone-in pork loin chops

Direction:
1. Take a small pan and mix preserves with chipotle pepper sauce on medium heat.
2. Keep ¼ cup of this sauce aside and rub the remaining over the pork.
3. Sprinkle salt over the pork and mix well.
4. Prepare and preheat the Ninja Foodi Grill on High-temperature setting.
5. Once it is preheated, open the lid and place 2 pork chops in the grill.
6. Cover the Ninja Foodi Grill's lid and grill them on the "Grilling Mode" for 5 minutes per side.
7. Serve with the reserved sauce.
8. Enjoy.

Nutrition: Calories 609 Total Fat 50.5 g Saturated Fat 11.7 g Cholesterol 58 mg Sodium 463 mg Total Carbs 9.9 g Fiber 1.5 g Sugar 0.3 g Protein 29.3 g

Cheese Burgers

Preparation Time: 10 minutes   **Cooking Time:** 20 minutes

Serving: 2

Ingredients :
- ¼ cup shredded cheddar cheese
- 3 tablespoons chili sauce, divided
- ½ tablespoon chili powder
- ½ lb. ground beef
- To serve:
- Lettuce leaves, mayonnaise, tomato slices
- 2 hamburger buns, split

Direction:

1. First, take all the ingredients for patties in a bowl.
2. Thoroughly mix them together then make 2 of the ½ inch patties out of it.
3. Prepare and preheat the Ninja Foodi Grill in a High-temperature setting.
4. Once it is preheated, open the lid and place 2 patties on the grill.
5. Cover the Ninja Foodi Grill's lid and grill them on the "Grilling Mode" for 5 minutes per side.
6. Serve with buns, lettuce, tomato, and mayonnaise.

Nutrition:
Calories 537 Total Fat 19.8 g Saturated Fat 1.4 g Cholesterol 10 mg Sodium 719 mg Total Carbs 25.1 g Fiber 0.9 g Sugar 1.4 g Protein 37.8 g

American Burger

Preparation Time: 10 minutes   **Cooking Time:** 20 minutes
Serving: 4
Ingredients :
- 1/2 cup bread crumbs
- 1/2 teaspoon pepper
- 1 large egg, whisked
- 1/2 teaspoon salt
- 4 seed hamburger buns, cut in half
- 1-lb. ground beef
- 1 tablespoon olive oil

Direction:
1. Take all the ingredients for a burger in a suitable bowl except the oil and the buns.
2. Mix them thoroughly together and make 4 of the ½ inch patties.
3. Brush these patties with olive oil.
4. Prepare and preheat the Ninja Foodi Grill on a High-temperature setting.
5. Once it is preheated, open the lid and place 2 patties in the grill.
6. Cover the Ninja Foodi Grill's lid and grill them on the "Grilling Mode" for 5 minutes per side until al dente.
7. Grill the remaining two patties in the same way.
8. Serve with buns.

Nutrition: Calories 301 Total Fat 15.8 g Saturated Fat 2.7 g Cholesterol 75 mg Sodium 389 mg Total Carbs 11.7 g Fiber 0.3g Sugar 0.1 g Protein 28.2 g

Basil Pizzas

Preparation Time: 10 minutes   **Cooking Time:** 17 minutes

Serving: 4

Ingredients :
- 4 (4 oz. Italian sausage, sliced
- 1 cup tomato basil pasta sauce
- 1/2 cup Parmesan cheese, grated
- 4 flatbreads
- 1/4 cup olive oil
- 2 cups mozzarella cheese, shredded
- 1/2 cup fresh basil, thinly sliced

Direction:
1. Prepare and preheat the Ninja Foodi Grill on a High-temperature setting.
2. Once it is preheated, open the lid and place the sliced sausages on the grill.
3. Cover the Ninja Foodi Grill's lid and grill them on the "Grilling Mode" for 3 minutes per side.
4. Now grill the flatbreads after rubbing with the oil for 3 minutes per side.
5. Top the bread with sauce, sausages, basil, and cheese.
6. Again, place the bread in the Ninja Foodi Grill and cover the lid.
7. Cook on Baking mode for 5 minutes on low-temperature settings.
8. Slice and serve.

Nutrition:
Calories 308 Total Fat 20.5 g Saturated Fat 3 g Cholesterol 42 mg Sodium 688 mg Total Carbs 40.3 g Sugar 1.4 g Fiber 4.3 g Protein 49 g

Skewers with Chimichurri

Preparation Time: 10 minutes   **Cooking Time:** 20 minutes
Serving: 6

Ingredients :

- 1/3 cup fresh cilantro
- 1/3 cup fresh parsley
- Juice of 1/2 lemon
- 1/3 cup fresh basil
- 1 tablespoon red wine vinegar
- 1 garlic clove, minced
- 1 shallot, minced
- 1/2 teaspoon crushed red pepper flakes
- 1/2 cup olive oil, divided
- Salt to taste
- Freshly ground Black pepper to taste
- 1 red onion, cubed
- 1 red pepper, cubed
- 1 orange pepper, cubed
- 1 yellow pepper, cubed
- 1 1/2 lb. sirloin steak, fat trimmed and diced

Direction:

1. First, take basil, parsley, vinegar, lemon juice, red pepper, shallots, garlic, and cilantro in a blender jug.
2. Blend well, then add ¼ cup olive oil, salt, and pepper and mix again.
3. Now thread the steak, peppers, and onion on the skewers.
4. Drizzle salt, black pepper, and remaining oil over the skewers.
5. Prepare and preheat the Ninja Foodi Grill on a High-temperature setting.
6. Once it is preheated, open the lid and place four skewers on the grill.
7. Cover the Ninja Foodi Grill's lid and grill them on the "Grilling Mode" for 5 minutes per side.
8. Grill the skewers in a batch until all are cooked.
9. Serve warm with green sauce.

Nutrition:

Calories 231 Total Fat 20.1 g Saturated Fat 2.4 g Cholesterol 110 mg Sodium 941 mg Total Carbs 20.1 g Fiber 0.9 g Sugar 1.4 g

Lamb Skewers

Preparation Time: 10 minutes   **Cooking Time:** 16 minutes
Serving: 8
Ingredients :

- 2 garlic cloves, minced
- 1 10 oz. pack couscous
- 1 tablespoon and 1 teaspoon cumin
- Juice of 2 lemons
- 1 1/2 cup yogurt
- Salt to taste
- 1 1/2 lb. lamb leg, boneless, cubed
- Freshly ground black pepper to taste
- 2 tomatoes, seeded and diced
- 1/2 small red onion, finely chopped
- 3 tablespoon olive oil
- 1/2 cucumber, seeded, and diced
- 1/4 cup finely chopped fresh parsley
- 1/4 cup finely chopped fresh mint
- Lemon wedges, to serve

Direction:
1. First, cook the couscous as per the given instructions on the package then fluff with a fork.
2. Whisk yogurt with garlic, cumin, lemon juice, salt, and black pepper in a large bowl.
3. Add lamb and mix well to coat the meat.
4. Separately toss red onion with cucumber, tomatoes, parsley, mint, lemon juice, olive oil, salt, and couscous in salad bowl.
5. Thread the seasoned lamb on 8 skewers and drizzle salt and black pepper over them.
6. Prepare and preheat the Ninja Foodi Grill in a High-temperature setting.
7. Once it is preheated, open the lid and place 4 lamb skewers on the grill.
8. Cover the Ninja Foodi Grill's lid and grill them on the "Grilling Mode" for 4 minutes per side.
9. Cook the remaining skewers in a similar way.
10. Serve warm with prepared couscous.

Nutrition:
Calories 472 Total Fat 11.1 g Saturated Fat 5.8 g Cholesterol 610 mg Sodium 749 mg Total Carbs 19.9 g Fiber 0.2 g Sugar 0.2 g Protein 13.5 g

Korean Flank Steak

Preparation Time: 10 minutes   **Cooking Time:** 12 minutes

Serving: 4

Ingredients :
- 1 teaspoon red pepper flakes
- 1/2 cup and 1 tablespoon soy sauce
- 1 1/2 lb. flank steak
- 1/4 cup and 2 tablespoon vegetable oil
- 1/2 cup rice wine vinegar
- 3 tablespoon Sriracha
- 2 cucumbers, seeded and sliced
- 4 cloves garlic, minced
- 2 tablespoon freshly minced ginger
- 2 tablespoon honey
- 3 tablespoon sesame oil
- 1 teaspoon sugar
- Salt to taste

Direction:
1. Mix ½ cup soy sauce, half of the rice wine, honey, ginger, garlic, 2 tablespoon Sriracha sauce, 2 tablespoon sesame oil, and vegetable oil in a large bowl.
2. Pour half of this sauce over the steak and rub it well.
3. Cover the steak and marinate for 10 minutes.
4. For salad mix remaining rice wine vinegar, sesame oil, sugar, red pepper flakes, Sriracha sauce, soy sauce, and salt in a salad bowl.
5. Prepare and preheat the Ninja Foodi Grill on High-temperature setting.
6. Once it is preheated, open the lid and place the steak in the grill.
7. Cover the Ninja Foodi Grill's lid and let it grill on the "Grilling Mode" for 6 minutes per side.
8. Slice and serve with cucumber salad.

Nutrition:
Calories 327 Total Fat 3.5 g Saturated Fat 0.5 g Cholesterol 162 mg Sodium 142 mg Total Carbs 33.6 g Fiber 0.4 g Sugar 0.5 g Protein 24.5 g

Fajita Skewers

Preparation Time: 10 minutes   **Cooking Time:** 14 minutes
Serving: 8

Ingredients:
- 1 bunch scallions, cut into large pieces
- 4 large bell peppers, cubed
- 1 lb. sirloin steak, cubed
- olive oil, for drizzling
- 1 pack tortillas, torn
- Salt to taste
- Ground black pepper to taste

Direction:
1. Thread the steak, tortillas, peppers, and scallions on the skewers.
2. Drizzle salt, black pepper, and olive oil over the skewers.
3. Prepare and preheat the Ninja Foodi Grill on the medium temperature setting.
4. Once it is preheated, open the lid and place 4 skewers on the grill.
5. Cover the Ninja Foodi Grill's lid and grill them on the "Grilling Mode" for 7 minutes.
6. Continue rotating the skewers every 2 minutes.
7. Cook the skewers in batches until all are grilled.
8. Serve warm.

Nutrition:
Calories 353 Total Fat 7.5 g Saturated Fat 1.1 g Cholesterol 20 mg Sodium 297 mg Total Carbs 10.4 g Fiber 0.2 g Sugar 0.1 g Protein 13.1 g

CHICKEN & TURKEY

Chicken Fajitas

Preparation Time: 10 minutes   **Cooking Tim e :** 15 minutes
Serving: 4

Ingredients :
- 4 boneless, skinless chicken breasts, sliced
- 1 small red onion, sliced
- 2 red bell peppers, sliced
- ½ cup spicy ranch salad dressing, divided
- ½ teaspoon dried oregano
- 8 corn tortillas
- 2 cups torn butter lettuce
- avocados, peeled and chopped

Directions:
1. Insert the Crisper Basket, and close the hood. Select AIR CRISP, set the temperature to 165°F, and set the time to 15 minutes. Select START/STOP to begin preheating.
2. Place the chicken, onion, and pepper in the air fryer basket. Drizzle with 1 tablespoon of the salad dressing and add the oregano. Toss to combine.
3. Air Frying. Grill for 10 to 14 minutes or until the chicken is 165°F on a food thermometer. Transfer the chicken and vegetables to a bowl and toss with the remaining salad dressing. Serve the chicken mixture with the tortillas, lettuce, and avocados and let everyone make their own creations.

Nutrition: Calories 783   Fat 38 g   Protein 72 g   Fiber 12 g

Balsamic-Rosemary Chicken Breasts

Preparation Time: 5 minutes   **Cooking Time:** 6 minutes

Serving: 4

Ingredients :
- ½ cup balsamic vinegar
- 2 tablespoons olive oil
- 2 rosemary sprigs, coarsely chopped
- 2 pounds boneless, skinless chicken breasts, pounded to ½-inch thickness

Directions :
1. Combine the balsamic vinegar, olive oil, and rosemary in a shallow baking dish. Add the chicken breasts and turn to coat. Cover with plastic wrap and refrigerate for at least 30 minutes or overnight.
2. Insert the Grill Grate and close the hood. Select GRILL, set the temperature to HIGH, and set the time to 6 minutes. Select START/STOP to begin preheating.
3. When the unit beeps to signify it has preheated, place the s chicken breasts on the Grill Grate. Close the hood and cook for 6 minutes until they have taken on grill marks and are cooked through.

Nutrition: Calories 299   Fat 20 g   Protein 52 g

Orange Curried Chicken Stir-Fry

Preparation Time: 10 minutes   **Cooking Time:** 18 minutes

Serving: 4

Ingredients :
- ¾ pound boneless, skinless chicken thighs, cut into 1-inch pieces
- 1 yellow bell pepper, cut into 1½-inch pieces
- 1 small red onion, sliced
- Olive oil for misting
- ¼ cup chicken stock
- 2 tablespoons honey
- ¼ cup orange juice
- 1 tablespoon cornstarch
- 2 to 3 teaspoons curry powder

Directions:

1. Insert the Crisper Basket, and close the hood. Select AIR CRISP, set the temperature to 165°F, and set the time to 15 minutes. Select START/STOP to begin preheating.
2. Put the chicken thighs, pepper, and red onion in the air fryer basket and mist with olive oil.
3. Air Frying. Cook for 12 to 15 minutes or until the chicken is cooked to 165°F, shaking the basket halfway through cooking time.
4. Remove the chicken and vegetables from the air fryer basket and set aside.
5. In a 6-inch metal bowl, combine the stock, honey, orange juice, cornstarch, and curry powder, and mix well. Add the chicken and vegetables, stir, and put the bowl in the basket.
6. Return the basket to the air fryer and cook for 2 minutes. Remove and stir, then cook for 2 to 3 minutes or until the sauce is thickened and bubbly.

Chicken Paillards With Fresh Tomato Sauce

Preparation Time: 5 minutes   **Cooking Time:** 4 minutes
Serving: 4

Ingredients :
- 2 whole skinless, boneless chicken breasts (each 12 to 16 ounces, or 4 half breasts (each half 6 to 8 ounces
- 1 clove garlic, minced
- 3 fresh basil leaves, minced, plus 4 basil sprigs for garnish
- Coarse salt (kosher or sea and freshly ground black pepper
- 2 tablespoons extra-virgin olive oil
- TOMATO SAUCE
- 1 clove garlic, minced
- ½ teaspoon salt, or more to taste
- 1 large ripe red tomato (6 to 8 ounces, seeded (**see Tips** and cut into ¼-inch dice
- 12 niçoise olives, or 6 black olives, pitted and cut into ¼-inch dice
- 8 fresh basil leaves, thinly slivered
- ¼ cup extra-virgin olive oil
- 1 tablespoon red wine vinegar, or more to taste
- Freshly ground black pepper

Directions :
1. If using whole chicken breasts, divide them in half. Trim any sinews or excess fat off the chicken breasts and discard. Remove the tenders from the breasts and set aside. Rinse the breasts under cold running water, then drain. Place a breast half between 2 pieces of plastic wrap and gently pound it to a thickness of between ¼ and ⅛ inch using a meat pounder, the side of a heavy cleaver, a rolling pin, or the bottom of a heavy saucepan. Repeat with the remaining breast halves.

2. Place the garlic and minced basil, ½ teaspoon of salt, and ½ teaspoon of pepper in a bowl and mash to a paste with the back of a spoon. Stir in the olive oil. Brush each paillard on both sides with the garlic and basil mixture and season lightly with salt and pepper.
3. Insert the Grill Grate and close the hood. Select GRILL, set the temperature to HIGH, and set the time to 4 minutes. Select START/STOP to begin preheating.
4. When the unit beeps to signify it has preheated, place the paillards on the Grill Grate. Close the hood and cook for 4 minutes.Use the poke test to check for doneness; the chicken should feel firm when pressed. You may need to work in more than one batch; cover the grilled paillards with aluminum foil to keep warm until ready to serve.
5. Place the garlic and salt in a nonreactive bowl and mash to a paste with the back of a spoon. Add the tomato, olives, basil, olive oil, and vinegar and stir to mix. Taste for seasoning, adding more salt and/or vinegar as necessary and pepper to taste; the sauce should be highly seasoned. Transfer the paillards to a platter or plates and spoon Tomato Sauce over them. Garnish each with a sprig of basil and serve at once.

Grilled Chicken Fajitas

Preparation Time: 5 minutes   **Cooking Time:** 6 minutes

Serving: 6

Ingredients :
- CHICKEN
- ¼ cup olive oil, divided
- juice from 1 lime
- 3 large boneless skinless chicken breasts, butterflied
- 1 each red, yellow, and orange peppers
- 1 medium Vidalia onion
- a pinch of salt
- 12 small soft flour tortillas
- SEASONING
- 1½ Tbsp. chili powder
- 2 tsp. ground cumin
- 2 tsp. kosher salt
- 2 tsp. smoked paprika
- 1 tsp. ground cinnamon
- 1 tsp. onion powder
- 1 tsp. garlic powder
- 1 tsp. cayenne pepper
- ½ tsp. white sugar
- zest from 1 lime

Directions :
1. Insert the Grill Grate and close the hood. Select GRILL, set the temperature to HIGH, and set the time to 4 minutes. Select START/STOP to begin preheating.
2. Combine all the seasoning ingredients into small bowl and whisk together.
3. Whisk 2 tablespoons olive oil and the lime juice together in medium mixing bowl. Add butterflied chicken breasts. Toss to evenly coat.
4. Evenly sprinkle seasoning on both sides of chicken, ensuring uniform coverage.

5. Thinly slice peppers and onion. In a large mixing bowl, toss sliced vegetables with remaining 2 tablespoons of olive oil and a pinch of salt.
6. When the unit beeps to signify it has preheated, place the vegetables on the Grill Grate. Close the hood and cook for 4 minutes.
7. As veggies near completion, place seasoned chicken on grill. Close the hood and cook for 4 minutes.
8. Remove both meat and vegetables from the grill, slice chicken into thin strips, and keep warm.
9. Toss flour tortillas on grill for 15 to 30 seconds per side, just to warm them up and slightly toast them. Don't cook them to the point that they are no longer flexible. Serve hot with toppings of your choice: cheese, fresh limes, sour cream, cilantro, and so on.

Honey-Mustard Chicken Tenders

Preparation Time: 5 minutes   **Cooking Time:** 3 minutes
Serving: 4
Ingredients :
- ½ cup Dijon mustard
- 2 tablespoons honey
- 2 tablespoons olive oil
- 1 teaspoon freshly ground black pepper
- 2 pounds chicken tenders
- ½ cup walnuts

Directions :
1. Whisk together the mustard, honey, olive oil, and pepper in a medium bowl. Add the chicken and toss to coat.
2. Finely grind the walnuts by pulsing them in a food processor or putting them in a heavy-duty plastic bag and pounding them with a rolling pin or heavy skillet.
3. Insert the Grill Grate and close the hood. Select GRILL, set the temperature to HIGH, and set the time to 4 minutes. Select START/STOP to begin preheating.
4. Toss the chicken tenders in the ground walnuts to coat them lightly.
5. Grill the chicken tenders for about 3 minutes, until they have taken on grill marks and are cooked through. Serve hot, at room temperature, or refrigerate and serve cold.

Nutrition: Calories 444   Fat 20 g   Protein 6 g

Chicken Roast with Pineapple Salsa

Preparation Time: 10 minutes   **Cooking Time:** 45 minutes   **Serving:** 2

Ingredients :
- ¼ cup extra virgin olive oil
- ¼ cup freshly chopped cilantro
- 1 avocado, diced
- 1-pound boneless chicken breasts
- 2 cups canned pineapples
- 2 teaspoons honey
- Juice from 1 lime
- Salt and pepper to taste

Directions:
1. Insert the Crisper Basket, and close the hood. Select AIR CRISP, set the temperature to 390°F, and set the time to 45 minutes. Select START/STOP to begin preheating. Place the grill pan accessory in the air fryer, season the chicken breasts with lime juice, olive oil, honey, salt, and pepper.
2. Air Frying. Place on the grill pan and cook for 45 minutes and flip the chicken every 10 minutes to grill all sides evenly.
3. Once the chicken is cooked, serve with pineapples, cilantro, and avocado.

Nutrition:
Calories 744   Fat 33 g Protein 5 g

Mustard Chicken Tenders

Preparation Time: 5 minutes   **Cooking Time:** 20 minutes   **Serving:** 4

Ingredients :
- ½ C. coconut flour
- 1 tbsp. spicy brown mustard
- 2 beaten eggs
- 1 pound of chicken tenders

Directions:
1. Insert the Crisper Basket, and close the hood. Select AIR CRISP, set the temperature to 390°F, and set the time to 20 minutes. Select START/STOP to begin preheating.Season tenders with pepper and salt.
2. Place a thin layer of mustard onto tenders and then dredge in flour and dip in egg. Air Frying.
3. Add to the air fryer basket, set temperature to 390°F, and set time to 20 minutes.

Nutrition:
Calories 404   Fat 20 g   Protein 22 g   Sugar 4 g

Tarragon Chicken Tenders

Preparation Time: 5 minutes   **Cooking Time:** 5 minutes

Serving: 4

Ingredients :

- FOR THE CHICKEN:
- 1½ pounds chicken tenders (12 to 16 tenders
- Coarse salt (kosher or sea and freshly ground black pepper
- 3 tablespoons chopped fresh tarragon leaves, plus 4 whole sprigs for garnish
- 1 teaspoon finely grated lemon zest
- 2 tablespoons fresh lemon juice
- 2 tablespoons extra-virgin olive oil
- FOR THE SAUCE (OPTIONAL:
- 2 tablespoons fresh lemon juice
- 2 tablespoons salted butter
- ½ cup heavy (whipping cream

Directions :

1. Make the chicken: Place the chicken tenders in a nonreactive baking dish just large enough to hold them in a single layer. Season the tenders generously on both sides with salt and pepper. Sprinkle the chopped tarragon and lemon zest all over the tenders, patting them onto the chicken with your fingertips. Drizzle the lemon juice and the olive oil over the tenders and pat them onto the chicken. Let the tenders marinate in the refrigerator, covered, for 10 minutes.
2. Drain the chicken tenders well by lifting one end with tongs and letting the marinade drip off. Discard the marinade.Insert the Grill Grate and close the hood. Select GRILL, set the temperature to HIGH, and set the time to 4 minutes. Select START/STOP to begin preheating.
3. Place the chicken tenders on the hot grill, then close the lid. The chicken tenders will be done after cooking 3 to 5 minutes. Use the poke test to check for doneness; the chicken should feel firm when pressed. You may need to cook the chicken in more than one batch; cover the grilled tenders with aluminum foil to keep warm until ready to serve.
4. Transfer the chicken tenders to a platter or plates. If making the sauce, place the lemon juice and the butter in a small saucepan or in the grill pan over medium heat. Add the cream and bring to a boil (use a wooden spoon to scrape up the brown bits from between the ridges of the grill pan. Let the sauce boil until thickened, 3 to 5 minutes. Pour the lemon cream sauce over the chicken tenders and serve at once.

Cheesy Chicken in Leek-Tomato Sauce

Preparation Time: 10 minutes   **Cooking Time:** 20 minutes

Serving: 4

Ingredients :
- 2 large-sized chicken breasts, cut in half lengthwise
- Salt and ground black pepper, to taste
- 4 ounces Cheddar cheese, cut into sticks
- 1 tablespoon sesame oil
- 1 cup leeks, chopped
- 2 cloves garlic, minced
- 2/3 cup roasted vegetable stock
- 2/3 cup tomato puree
- 1 teaspoon dried rosemary
- 1 teaspoon dried thyme

Directions:
1. Insert the Crisper Basket, and close the hood. Select AIR CRISP, set the temperature to 390°F, and set the time to 15 minutes. Select START/STOP to begin preheating.
2. Firstly, season chicken breasts with the salt and black pepper; place a piece of Cheddar cheese in the middle. Then, tie it using a kitchen string; drizzle with sesame oil and reserve.
3. Add the leeks and garlic to the oven safe bowl.
4. Air Frying.
5. Cook in the air fryer at 390 degrees F for 5 minutes or until tender.
6. Add the reserved chicken. Throw in the other ingredients and cook for 12 to 13 minutes more or until the chicken is done. Enjoy!

Honey BBQ-Glazed Chicken Drumsticks

Preparation Time: 5 minutes   **Cooking Time:** 45 minutes
Serving: 5

Ingredients :
- 10 to 12 chicken legs
- 2 Tbsp. baking powder
- ½ Tbsp. kosher salt
- olive oil spray
- 2 Tbsp. BBQ rub, plus 1 tsp. for glaze
- 3 Tbsp. honey

Directions :
1. Remove chicken from its packaging. Rinse and pat dry with a paper towel.
2. Mix together baking powder and salt in a shaker bottle and dust over the drumsticks. You want to be sure you coat the skin lightly and evenly; this is essential to dry out the skin, which will allow for the skin to get crispy on the grill.
3. Place chicken in refrigerator for at least 1 to 2 hours to allow the baking powder and salt to pull the moisture out of the skin.
4. Insert the Grill Grate and close the hood. Select GRILL, set the temperature to HIGH, and set the time to 45 minutes. Select START/STOP to begin preheating.
5. Spray drumsticks lightly with olive oil spray and generously coat with BBQ rub.
6. Place the drumsticks in a roasting rack. Place the rack in the Grill Grate and close the hood. Allow chicken to cook for about 45 minutes or until internal temperature is 165°F.
7. Remove chicken from grill and pour juices from drip pan into saucepan. Place saucepan over medium heat for 5 minutes while whisking in honey and 1 teaspoon BBQ rub.
8. Using a brush, glaze drumsticks with honey mixture, Garnish and serve.

Marinated Turkey Breast With Cranberry Compote

Preparation Time: 5 minutes   **Cooking Time:** 4 minutes

Serving: 6

Ingredients :
- CRANBERRY COMPOTE
- ½ cup sugar
- ½ cup water
- 1 (12-ounce bag fresh or frozen cranberries
- Grated zest and juice of 1 orange
- 1 tablespoon ketchup
- TURKEY
- ¼ cup olive oil
- ¼ cup pure maple syrup
- 8 fresh thyme sprigs or 1 teaspoon dried thyme
- 2 whole cloves
- ¾ teaspoon salt
- ½ teaspoon freshly ground black pepper
- 6 (6-ounce boneless, skinless turkey breast cutlets pounded to ½-inch thickness
- ½ cup walnut pieces

Directions :
1. CRANBERRY COMPOTE
2. In a medium saucepan, combine the sugar and water. Over medium heat, stir until the sugar has dissolved, about 2 minutes. Add the cranberries, orange zest and juice, and ketchup, and bring to a boil. When the mixture begins to bubble, lower the heat and continue to stir until the berries begin to pop and sauce begins to thicken, about 15 minutes. Transfer to a serving bowl. Let cool to room temperature. (The compote can be covered with plastic wrap and refrigerated overnight. Bring to room temperature before serving.
3. TURKEYIn a large shallow baking dish or bowl, combine the olive oil, maple syrup, thyme, cloves, salt, and pepper. Add the turkey cutlets and turn to coat. Cover with plastic wrap and refrigerate for at least 2 hours or overnight.
4. Insert the Grill Grate and close the hood. Select GRILL, set the temperature to HIGH, and set the time to 4 minutes. Select START/STOP to begin preheating.
5. Grill the turkey cutlets for about 3 minutes, until they have taken on grill marks and are cooked through.
6. Transfer to serving plates, top with the cranberry compote, sprinkle with the walnuts, and serve immediately.

Grilled Chicken With Salsa Criolla

Preparation Time: 5 minutes   **Cooking Time:** 6 minutes

Serving: 5

Ingredients :
- 8 chicken thighs, with skin and bones (about 2 pounds total
- 1 tablespoon extra-virgin olive oil
- Coarse salt (kosher or sea and freshly ground or cracked black peppercorns
- About 1 tablespoon dried oregano
- SALSA CRIOLLA
- 1 luscious ripe red tomato, seeded (but not peeled and cut into ¼-inch dice
- 1 small or ½ large red bell pepper, seeded and cut into ¼-inch dice
- 1 small or ½ medium-size onion, cut into ¼-inch dice
- 1 tablespoon finely chopped fresh flat-leaf parsley
- ¼ cup extra-virgin olive oil
- 2 tablespoons red wine vinegar
- Coarse salt (kosher or sea and freshly ground black pepper

Directions :
1. Rinse the thighs under cold running water, then drain and blot dry with paper towels. Place a thigh on a work surface skin side down. Using a sharp paring knife, cut along the length of the thigh bone. Cut the meat away from one end of the bone, then pull or scrape the meat from the bone. Cut the meat away from the other end of the bone. Repeat with the remaining thighs. Discard the bones or set them aside for making stock or another use.
2. Lightly brush the chicken thighs all over with olive oil, then season them generously with salt, pepper, and oregano.
3. Insert the Grill Grate and close the hood. Select GRILL, set the temperature to HIGH, and set the time to 6 minutes. Select START/STOP to begin preheating.
4. When the unit beeps to signify it has preheated, place the chicken thighs on the Grill Grate. Close the hood and cook for 6 minutes.
5. Use the poke test to check for doneness; the chicken should feel firm when pressed.Place the tomato, bell pepper, onion, parsley, olive oil, and vinegar in an attractive nonreactive serving bowl and toss to mix. Season with salt and pepper to taste. The sauce can be made several hours ahead.
6. Transfer the chicken thighs to a platter or plates and serve at once with the Salsa Criolla on top or on the side.

Chicken BBQ with Sweet And Sour Sauce

Preparation Time: 5 minutes   **Cooking Time:** 40 minutes

Serving: 6

Ingredients :
- ¼ cup minced garlic
- ¼ cup tomato paste
- ¾ cup minced onion
- ¾ cup sugar
- 1 cup soy sauce
- 1 cup water
- 1 cup white vinegar
- 6 chicken drumsticks
- Salt and pepper to taste

Directions:
1. Place all Ingredients in a Ziploc bag
2. Allow to marinate for at least 2 hours in the fridge.
3. Insert the Crisper Basket, and close the hood. Select AIR CRISP, set the temperature to 390°F, and set the time to 40 minutes. Select START/STOP to begin preheating.
4. Place the grill pan accessory in the air fryer.
5. Air Frying. Grill the chicken for 40 minutes.
6. Flip the chicken every 10 minutes for even grilling.
7. Meanwhile, pour the marinade in a saucepan and heat over medium flame until the sauce thickens.
8. Before serving the chicken, brush with the glaze.

Nutrition: Calories 460   Fat 20 g   Protein 28 g   Sugar 3 g

Ricotta and Parsley Stuffed Turkey Breasts

Preparation Time: 5 minutes   **Cooking Time:** 25 minutes

Serving: 4

Ingredients :
- 1 turkey breast, quartered
- 1 cup Ricotta cheese
- 1/4 cup fresh Italian parsley, chopped
- 1 teaspoon garlic powder
- 1/2 teaspoon cumin powder
- 1 egg, beaten
- 1 teaspoon paprika
- Salt and ground black pepper, to taste
- Crushed tortilla chips
- 1 ½ tablespoons extra-virgin olive oil

Directions:
1. Firstly, flatten out each piece of turkey breast with a rolling pin. Prepare three mixing bowls.
2. In a shallow bowl, combine Ricotta cheese with the parsley, garlic powder, and cumin powder.
3. Place the Ricotta/parsley mixture in the middle of each piece. Repeat with the remaining pieces of the turkey breast and roll them up.
4. In another shallow bowl, whisk the egg together with paprika. In the third shallow bowl, combine the salt, pepper, and crushed tortilla chips.
5. Dip each roll in the whisked egg, then, roll them over the tortilla chips mixture.
6. Insert the Crisper Basket, and close the hood. Select AIR CRISP, set the temperature to 350°F, and set the time to 25 minutes. Select START/STOP to begin preheating.
7. Transfer prepared rolls to the air fryer basket. Drizzle olive oil over all.
8. Air frying. Cook at 350 degrees F for 25 minutes, working in batches. Serve warm, garnished with some extra parsley, if desired.

Sweet Thai Cilantro Chili Chicken Quarters

Preparation Time: 5 minutes   **Cooking Time:** 5 minutes

Serving: 5

Ingredients :
- 4 chicken leg quarters, lightly coated with olive oil
- 1 cup and 1 tsp. water
- ¾ cup rice vinegar
- ½ cup white sugar
- 3 Tbsp. freshly chopped cilantro
- 2 Tbsp. freshly minced ginger root
- 2 tsp. freshly minced garlic
- 2 Tbsp. crushed red pepper flakes
- 2 Tbsp. ketchup
- 2 Tbsp. cornstarch
- 2 Tbsp. fresh basil chiffonade ("chiffonade" is fancy for "thinly sliced"

Directions :
1. Insert the Grill Grate and close the hood. Select GRILL, set the temperature to HIGH, and set the time to 8 minutes. Select START/STOP to begin preheating.
2. In a medium-sized saucepan, bring 1 cup water and the vinegar to a boil over high heat.
3. Stir in sugar, cilantro, ginger, garlic, red pepper flakes, and ketchup; simmer for 5 minutes.
4. In small mixing bowl, mix together 1 teaspoon warm water and 2 tablespoons cornstarch. Use a fork for mixing this, and what you'll end up with will resemble white school glue.
5. Slowly whisk the cornstarch mixture into the simmering sauce, and continue mixing until sauce thickens. Set aside.
6. When the unit beeps to signify it has preheated, place the chicken quarters skin side down on the Grill Grate. Close the hood and cook for 8 minutes.
7. At 155°F internal temperature, glaze chicken with sauce and allow to finish cooking to an internal temperature of 165°F.
8. Plate, garnish with basil, and serve.

Cheesy Turkey-Rice with Broccoli

Preparation Time: 5 minutes   **Cooking Time:** 20 minutes

Serving: 4

Ingredients :
- 1 cup cooked, chopped turkey meat
- 1 tablespoon and 1-1/2 teaspoons butter, melted
- 1/2 (10 ounce package frozen broccoli, thawed
- 1/2 (7 ounce package whole wheat crackers, crushed
- 1/2 cup shredded Cheddar cheese
- 1/2 cup uncooked white rice

Directions:

1. Insert the Crisper Basket, and close the hood. Select AIR CRISP, set the temperature to 360°F, and set the time to 15 minutes. Select START/STOP to begin preheating.
2. Bring to a boil 2 cups of water in a saucepan. Stir in rice and simmer for 20 minutes. Turn off fire and set aside.
3. Lightly grease baking pan of air fryer with cooking spray. Mix in cooked rice, cheese, broccoli, and turkey. Toss well to mix.
4. Mix well melted butter and crushed crackers in a small bowl. Evenly spread on top of rice.
5. Air Frying.
6. For 20 minutes, cook on 360°F until tops are lightly browned.
7. Serve and enjoy.

DESSERT

Blueberry Lemon Muffins

Preparation Time: 5 minutes   **Cooking Time:** 10 minutes

Serving: 12

Ingredients :
- 1 tsp. vanilla
- Juice and zest of 1 lemon
- 2 eggs
- 1 C. blueberries
- ½ C. cream
- ¼ C. avocado oil
- ½ C. monk fruit
- 2 ½ C. almond flour

Directions:
1. Mix monk fruit and flour together.In another bowl, mix vanilla, egg, lemon juice, and cream together. Add mixtures together and blend well.Spoon batter into cupcake holders.
2. Air Frying. Place in air fryer. Bake 10 minutes at 320 degrees, checking at 6 minutes to ensure you don't overbake them.

Nutrition:
Calories 317   Fat 11 g   Protein 3 g   Sugar 5 g

Grilled Pound Cake with Berry Compote

Preparation Time: 5 minutes   **Cooking Time:** 30 minutes

Serving: 4

Ingredients :
- FOR THE POUND CAKE
- 1 cup butter, softened
- 1 cup sugar
- 4 eggs
- 1 tsp. vanilla
- pinch of salt
- 2 cups flour
- FOR THE COMPOTE
- 1 cup fresh mixed berries (any variety
- ½ cup sugar
- 1 Tbsp. cornstarch

Directions :
1. Mix the compote ingredients together in a saucepan. Bring to a boil, stirring well. Remove from the heat, and set aside. In a mixing bowl, mix the butter and sugar until fluffy.
2. Add the eggs one at a time, mixing well between each egg. Add the vanilla and salt.
3. Stir in the flour until well combined, but do not overmix.
4. Scoop and level the pound cake batter out onto a sheet pan.
5. Bake until the cake is golden brown.
6. Once the pound cake is cooled, cut into 3-inch squares. Heat the grill to medium, and grill the pound cakes lightly. Serve warm with the compote drizzled over the top.

Sweet Cream Cheese Wontons

Preparation Time: 5 minutes   **Cooking Time:** 5 minutes   **Serving:** 16

Ingredients :
- 1 egg mixed with a bit of water
- Wonton wrappers
- ½ C. powdered erythritol
- 8 ounces softened cream cheese
- Olive oil

Directions:
1. Mix sweetener and cream cheese together.
2. Lay out 4 wontons at a time and cover with a dish towel to prevent drying out.
3. Place ½ of a teaspoon of cream cheese mixture into each wrapper.
4. Dip finger into egg/water mixture and fold diagonally to form a triangle. Seal edges well. Repeat with remaining ingredients.
5. Insert the Crisper Basket, and close the hood. Select AIR CRISP, set the temperature to 400°F, and set the time to 5 minutes. Select START/STOP to begin preheating. Air frying. Place filled wontons into the air fryer and cook 5 minutes at 400 degrees, shaking halfway through cooking.

Nutrition:
Calories 303   Fat 3 g   Protein 1 g   Sugar 4 g

Air Fryer Cinnamon Rolls

Preparation Time: 15 minutes   **Cooking Time:** 5 minutes   **Serving:** 8

Ingredients :
- 1 ½ tbsp. cinnamon
- ¾ C. brown sugar
- ¼ C. melted coconut oil
- 1 pound frozen bread dough, thawed
- Glaze:
- ½ tsp. vanilla
- 1 ¼ C. powdered erythritol
- 2 tbsp. softened ghee
- ounces softened cream cheese

Directions:
1. Lay out bread dough and roll out into a rectangle. Brush melted ghee over dough and leave a 1-inch border along edges.
2. Mix cinnamon and sweetener together and then sprinkle over dough.
3. Roll dough tightly and slice into 8 pieces. Let sit 1-2 hours to rise.
4. To make the glaze, simply mix ingredients together till smooth.
5. Air Frying. Once rolls rise, place into air fryer and cook 5 minutes at 350 degrees. Serve rolls drizzled in cream cheese glaze. Enjoy

Nutrition: Calories 390   Fat 8 g   Protein 1 g   Sugar 7 g

Smoked Apple Crumble

Preparation Time: 5 minutes   **Cooking Time:** 45 minutes

Serving: 4

Ingredients :

- Filling
- 4–5 large Honeycrisp apples, peeled and sliced
- juice from ½ lemon
- 2 Tbsp. flour
- ⅓ cup sugar
- 1 Tbsp. ground cinnamon
- 1 tsp. ground nutmeg
- Topping
- 1 cup brown sugar
- ½ cup flour
- ½ cup oatmeal
- ½ cup caramel baking chips
- ¼ cup candied pecans
- 1 Tbsp. ground cinnamon
- 1 tsp. baking powder
- ½ tsp. salt
- ½ cup salted butter, cold and cut into small chunks

Directions :

1. Insert the Grill Grate and close the hood. Select GRILL, set temperature to HIGH, and set time to 40 minutes. Select START/STOP to begin preheating.
2. Place apples in a large mixing bowl and toss with lemon juice. Then add in flour, sugar, cinnamon, and nutmeg, and mix thoroughly.
3. Pour apples into a greased cast-iron pan. Set mixture aside.
4. Using the now-empty mixing bowl, combine brown sugar, flour, oatmeal, caramel chips, pecans, cinnamon, baking powder, and salt for the topping.
5. Using a pastry blender or large fork, cut the cold butter into the topping mix.
6. Cover apples with topping mixture.
7. Add one or two pecan wood chunks to the hot coals. Place apple crumble over the Roasting Rack.
8. Close the hood and bake until apples start to bubble and topping begins to brown (about 45 minutes.
9. Remove from grill and serve warm with French vanilla ice cream.

Bread Pudding with Cranberry

Preparation Time: 5 minutes   **Cooking Time:** 35 minutes   **Serving:** 4

Ingredients :
- 1-1/2 cups milk
- 2-1/2 eggs
- 1/2 cup cranberries1 teaspoon butter
- 1/4 cup and 2 tablespoons white sugar
- 1/4 cup golden raisins
- 1/8 teaspoon ground cinnamon
- 3/4 cup heavy whipping cream
- 3/4 teaspoon lemon zest
- 3/4 teaspoon kosher salt
- 3/4 French baguettes, cut into 2-inch slices
- 3/8 vanilla bean, split and seeds scraped away

Directions:
1. Lightly grease baking pan of air fryer with cooking spray. Spread baguette slices, cranberries, and raisins. In blender, blend well vanilla bean, cinnamon, salt, lemon zest, eggs, sugar, and cream. Pour over baguette slices. Let it soak for an hour. Cover pan with foil.
2. For 35 minutes, cook on 330°F. Let it rest for 10 minutes. Serve and enjoy.

Nutrition:
Calories 590   Fat 25 g   Protein 17 g   Sugar 9 g

Black and White Brownies

Preparation Time: 10 minutes   **Cooking Time:** 20 minutes   **Serving:** 8

Ingredients :
- 1 egg
- ¼ cup brown sugar
- 2 tablespoons white sugar
- 2 tablespoons safflower oil
- 1 teaspoon vanilla
- ¼ cup cocoa powder
- ⅓ cup all-purpose flour
- ¼ cup white chocolate chips
- Nonstick baking spray with flour

Directions:
1. In a medium bowl, beat the egg with the brown sugar and white sugar. Beat in the oil and vanilla. Add the cocoa powder and flour, and stir just until combined. Fold in the white chocolate chips. Spray a 6-by-6-by-2-inch baking pan with nonstick spray. Spoon the brownie batter into the pan.
2. Bake for 20 minutes or until the brownies are set when lightly touched with a finger. Let cool for 30 minutes before slicing to serve.

French Toast Bites

Preparation Time: 5 minutes   **Cooking Time:** 15 minutes
Serving: 8
Ingredients :
- Almond milk
- Cinnamon
- Sweetener
- 3 eggs
- 4 pieces wheat bread

Directions:
1. Insert the Crisper Basket, and close the hood. Select AIR CRISP, set the temperature to 360°F, and set the time to 15 minutes. Select START/STOP to begin preheating. Whisk eggs and thin out with almond milk.
2. Mix 1/3 cup of sweetener with lots of cinnamon.
3. Tear bread in half, ball up pieces and press together to form a ball. Soak bread balls in egg and then roll into cinnamon sugar, making sure to thoroughly coat. Air frying. Place coated bread balls into the air fryer and bake 15 minutes.

Nutrition:
Calories 300   Fat 10 g   Protein 2 g   Sugar 4 g

Baked Apple

Preparation Time: 5 minutes   **Cooking Time:** 20 minutes
Serving: 4
Ingredients :
- ¼ C. water
- ¼ tsp. nutmeg
- ¼ tsp. cinnamon
- 1 ½ tsp. melted ghee
- 2 tbsp. raisins
- 2 tbsp. chopped walnuts
- 1 medium apple

Directions:
1. Insert the Crisper Basket, and close the hood. Select AIR CRISP, set the temperature to 350°F, and set the time to 20 minutes. Select START/STOP to begin preheating.
2. Slice apple in half and discard some of the flesh from the center.
3. Place into frying pan. Mix remaining ingredients together except water. Spoon mixture to the middle of apple halves. Pour water over filled apples.
4. Air frying. Place pan with apple halves into the air fryer, bake 20 minutes.

Nutrition :
Calories 205   Fat 11 g   Protein 2 g   Sugar 5 g

Coffee And Blueberry Cake

Preparation Time: 5 minutes   **Cooking Time:** 35 minutes

Serving: 6

Ingredients :
- 1 cup white sugar
- 1 egg
- 1/2 cup butter, softened
- 1/2 cup fresh or frozen blueberries
- 1/2 cup sour cream
- 1/2 teaspoon baking powder
- 1/2 teaspoon ground cinnamon
- 1/2 teaspoon vanilla extract
- 1/4 cup brown sugar
- 1/4 cup chopped pecans
- 1/8 teaspoon salt
- 1-1/2 teaspoons confectioners' sugar for dusting
- 3/4 cup and 1 tablespoon all-purpose flour

Directions:
1. In a small bowl, whisk well pecans, cinnamon, and brown sugar.
2. In a blender, blend well all wet Ingredients. Add dry Ingredients except for confectioner's sugar and blueberries. Blend well until smooth and creamy.
3. Lightly grease baking pan of air fryer with cooking spray.
4. Pour half of batter in pan. Sprinkle half of pecan mixture on top. Pour the remaining batter. And then topped with remaining pecan mixture.
5. Cover pan with foil.
6. For 35 minutes, cook on 330°F.
7. Serve and enjoy with a dusting of confectioner's sugar.

Nutrition: Calories 480   Fat 26 g   Protein 5 g   Sugar 8 g

Cinnamon Sugar Roasted Chickpeas

Preparation Time: 5 minutes   **Cooking Time:** 10 minutes

Serving: 2

Ingredients :
- 1 tbsp. sweetener
- 1 tbsp. cinnamon
- 1 C. chickpeas

Directions:
1. Insert the Crisper Basket, and close the hood. Select AIR CRISP, set the temperature to 390°F, and set the time to 10 minutes. Select START/STOP to begin preheating. Rinse and drain chickpeas.
2. Mix all ingredients together and add to air fryer. Air frying. Cook 10 minutes.

Nutrition: Calories 115   Fat 20 g   Protein 18 g   Sugar 7 g

Cinnamon Fried Bananas

Preparation Time: 5 minutes   **Cooking Time:** 10 minutes   **Serving:** 2-3

Ingredients :
- 1 C. panko breadcrumbs
- 3 tbsp. cinnamon
- ½ C. almond flour
- 3 egg whites
- 8 ripe bananas
- 3 tbsp. vegan coconut oil

Directions:
1. Heat coconut oil and add breadcrumbs. Mix around 2-3 minutes until golden. Pour into bowl. Peel and cut bananas in half. Roll each bananas half into flour, eggs, and crumb mixture.
2. Air Frying. Place into the air fryer. Cook 10 minutes at 280 degrees.
3. A great addition to a healthy banana split!

Nutrition: Calories 215 Fat 11 g Protein 5 g Sugar 5 g

Cherry-Choco Bars

Preparation Time: 5 minutes   **Cooking Time:** 15 minutes   **Serving:** 8

Ingredients :
- ¼ teaspoon salt
- ½ cup almonds, sliced
- ½ cup chia seeds
- ½ cup dark chocolate, chopped
- ½ cup dried cherries, chopped
- ½ cup prunes, pureed
- ½ cup quinoa, cooked
- ¾ cup almond butter
- 1/3 cup honey
- 2 cups old-fashioned oats
- 2 tablespoon coconut oil

Directions:
1. Insert the Crisper Basket, and close the hood. Select AIR CRISP, set the temperature to 375°F, and set the time to 15 minutes. Select START/STOP to begin preheating.
2. In a mixing bowl, combine the oats, quinoa, chia seeds, almond, cherries, and chocolate.
3. In a saucepan, heat the almond butter, honey, and coconut oil.
4. Pour the butter mixture over the dry mixture. Add salt and prunes.
5. Mix until well combined.
6. Pour over a baking dish that can fit inside the air fryer.
7. Air frying. Cook for 15 minutes.
8. Let it cool for an hour before slicing into bars.

Nutrition: Calories 330   Fat 15 g   Protein 7 g   Sugar 8 g